2

WHERE HE SPORTED AND PLAYED

JACK LYNCH

A Sporting Celebration

Liam Ó Tuama

BLACKWATER PRESS

Editor

Anna O Donovan

Assistant Editor

Sinéad Kelleher

Design & Layout/Cover

Liz Murphy

© Liam Ó Tuama 2000

ISBN 1 84131 472 2

Produced in Ireland by
Blackwater Press,
c/o Folens Publishers,
Hibernian Industrial Estate,
Greenhills Road,
Tallaght, Dublin 24.

Contents

Buíochas

Ba mhaith liom buíochas a ghabháil le gach éinne a thug cabhair dom an leabhar seo a chur le chéile, agus a roinn go fial a gcuid eolais liom ar shaol Jack Lynch.

I wish to place on record my appreciation and sincere thanks to all those who contributed to and so willingly provided material for this celebration of Jack Lynch's sporting career.

Special mention has to be accorded to:

Mick Dunne, Jim O'Sullivan, Donal Keenan and Tim Horgan for their major contributions.

John Lyons, Dick Stokes and Pat Stakelum for their support and encouragement.

Irish Examiner Publications, especially Lillian Caverley and Declan Ryan.

Irish Independent Publications, *Irish Press PLC*, Ian Lee, RTE, An Post.

Tim Cadogan and Kieran Wyse, Cork County Library and Tom Morrisson.

Jim Cronin and Frank Murphy, Cork County Board, GAA.

PJ Mehigan for permission to use his father's 'Carbery's' match reports.

Colman Doyle and Des Barry for their photographic expertise.

Mary O'Brien of Color-Foto, Eddie Lyons and MI McSweeney of *Inside Cork*.

Ted McCarthy, Finbarr O'Connell and all those who kindly provided photographs.

Finbarr Lynch for his wonderful memory and time so willingly given.

Con Murphy, Tom Woulfe of Civil Service and Tim O'Connor of Limerick.

John Stokes, a Limerickman in Dublin, who made research so enjoyable and productive.

Liam Ó Conaill for his assistance with the proof reading.

Eileen Lehane, an accomplished and patient typist.

Colin Jones, my 12-year-old grandson, for his computer skills.

Paddy Deasy and Tim Cramer for their invaluable support and advice in the compilation of this book.

Bouquets to:

John O'Connor and the staff at Blackwater Press for their advice and efficiency. A special word of thanks to Anna O Donovan, Editor, for her unfailing assistance and professionalism.

Buíochas fé leith:

A very special word of appreciation to Mrs Máirín Lynch for her wholehearted support of this publication.

My sincerest gratitude to Paddy Deasy and Tim Cramer for their assistance, advice and contributions. They played a major role in the preparation of this tribute to Jack Lynch.

At the request of Mrs Máirín Lynch, the royalties from the sale of this publication will go to the Cork Share Boys Charity.

It is with great pleasure that I welcome this book, *Where He Sported and Played*, compiled by Liam Ó Tuama of Glen Rovers, Jack's beloved club, and to which so many of his friends, on and off the field, contributed. Jack would have been extremely honoured, but he would never have wanted to be singled out in such a special way. Jack was a good hurler, but always said it was because he played with great hurlers.

I know that his dearest wish would be that the wonderful game of hurling would grow and expand into all of our counties, and particularly, that more and more of our young people would come to love and play this most ancient of our games which embodies the very spirit of Ireland.

My congratulations and deep appreciation to all the members of the GAA who contributed to this book and for remembering Jack in such a meaningful way.

Máirín Lynch.

Brollach

Tá an leabhar seo curtha le chéile chun gníomhartha Jack Lynch mar laoch spóirt a cheiliúradh. D'imir sé thar tréimhse fiche bliain agus is ar éigin go sárófar a éachtaí ar an bpáirc go deo.

Tugann an leabhar seo léargas dúinn ar na buanna agus tubaistí a bhí aige ar an bpáirc le linn na mblianta sin – ach pé duine a imir leis nó ina choinne ní raibh le rá acu ach gurb fhear uasal cineálta é Jack.

This book is a celebration of the sporting career of Jack Lynch. It covers the hurling and football exploits of an extraordinary sportsman who made his first competitive appearance at the age of 12.

His dedication to the games he played, and the skill and leadership he provided on the playing fields, brought honour to his school, club, county and province. His prowess remains unquestioned but, more importantly, his legacy of courageous, gentlemanly sportsmanship transcends all other considerations. It will remain as a beacon and an inspiration for generations of Gaelic sportsmen and sportswomen yet to come.

It is hoped that this book may help to relive glorious memories for the older generation and imbue in the young players of tomorrow those qualities of dedication, loyalty and honour which Jack Lynch so well epitomised.

Liam Ó Tuama.

Aitheasc an Uachtaráin

Is í mo phribhléid, mar Uachtarán Chumann Lúth Chleas Gael, fáiltiú roimh an bhfoilseachán seo. Cnuasach atá ann de thuairiscí ar éachtaí duine des na hÉireannaigh agus des na fir spóirt is mó riamh i gCumann Lúth Chleas Gael agus ina Chluichí Náisiúnta san fichiú aois. Is é an duine clúiteach seo ná Seán Ó Loinsigh.

The name of Jack Lynch is synonymous with all that is good in Gaelic games. He was renowned as an outstanding, skilful, competitive and sporting hurler and footballer in an era of many great players. Educated at the famed hurling nursery, North Monastery CBS, and a member of the Glen Rovers and St Nicholas clubs, Jack Lynch became a household name in the inter-county and inter-provincial arenas of hurling and football from 1935 to 1950, amassing many honours.

A natural leader, he was captain of the Cork hurlers in their heroic but narrowly unsuccessful All-Ireland bid in the famed 'Thunder and Lightning' final of 1939, but captained his county to victory in 1942. Jack Lynch was an inspiring figure in the Cork hurlers' four-in-a-row All-Ireland achievement of 1941 to 1944. This was to form only a part of an amazing personal and never surpassed record of six All-Ireland medals in a row, with Cork winning the 1945 football title and their hurlers again capturing the All-Ireland crown in 1946.

The Gaelic Athletic Association treasures Jack Lynch's marvellous contribution to the promotion and popularity of Gaelic Games. It is immensely proud that one of its most illustrious members was to portray the same high leadership qualities, integrity and vision, as he led this country as a most respected Taoiseach for almost a decade.

I applaud Glen Rovers' clubman, Liam Ó Tuama, on his timely initiative in compiling this wonderful chronicle of Jack Lynch's contribution to gaelic games at school, club, county and provincial level, and congratulate those who co-operated with him and contributed to this publication. May it inspire many young people in this country to follow in the footsteps of this truly great sporting gentleman.

Táim cinnte de go gcuirfear mór spéis ins an cnuasach seo. Is mó cuimhne thaitneamhach a mheabhróidh sé in aigne na mílte gan chuimse a chonaic é ag imirt, agus tabharfaidh sé léargas do a lán eile ar chrógacht agus ar chalmacht duine des na laochra is mó riamh i bpeil agus in iománaíocht.

Seán Mac Thaidhg.

Uachtarán Chumann Lúth Chleas Gael

Contributors

Mick Dunne was a most outstanding, respected and knowledgeable commentator with RTÉ. Previous to his career with RTE he was GAA correspondent for the *Irish Press*, where his reports on all important games were eagerly awaited.

Tim Horgan is the author of many GAA publications, including *Cork's Hurling Story* and *The Farna Story*. He is a teacher in Farrenferris College and is very much involved in the preparation of teams and the promotion of Gaelic games in the College.

PJ Mehigan, 'Carbery', a native of West Cork was one of the country's foremost journalists in the 1930s and '40s. His vivid description of games reported in the *Cork Weekly Examiner* brought them very much alive for his many readers. His *Carbery's Annual* was essential reading in many households at Christmas time. He had the further distinction of being a Radio Éireann commentator on Gaelic games in the 1930s.

Finbarr Lynch, a year older than his brother Jack, shared in many of his successes at underage level with the North Mon and Glen Rovers. An injury brought a premature end to his sporting career but his interest in sport continues to the present. He had a most successful career as a civil servant which spanned almost 50 years.

Jim O'Sullivan has been the leading *Irish Examiner* (formerly *The Cork Examiner*) GAA correspondent since the 1970s. He has been the recipient of many awards for his outstanding journalism.

Donal Keenan, a member of a family steeped in the GAA tradition, has been acknowledged over a long period as one of the outstanding Gaelic games journalists in the country. Having spent much of his career with Independent newspapers he is presently GAA correspondent for *Ireland on Sunday*.

———○———

Liam Ó Tuama has been a member of Glen Rovers and St Nicks clubs for over 50 years. He has won county championship medals in Junior, Intermediate and Senior Hurling. He played in goal on the Cork 1955 Junior Hurling team that won the All-Ireland Championship. An officer of Glen Rovers for over 20 years, he has served as Chairman, Vice-Chairman and Secretary. He compiled and edited the history of St Nicks football club, *The Nicks of Time* and the McNamee award-winning history of Glen Rovers, *The Spirit of the Glen*. He was a selector of the Cork Senior team that won the 1990 All-Ireland championship.

———○———

Tim Cramer is one of Cork's best-known journalists. He has had a number of books published and is a former editor and director of *The Cork Examiner*. He is a model railway enthusiast and a gardening fanatic. Tim is a prolific contributor to magazines which cater for his hobbies.

———○———

Paddy Deasy is a member and past officer of Glen Rovers club. He is the holder of Cork minor hurling and football County Championship medals. He was also involved in compiling *The Spirit of the Glen*. He is a former Assistant County Manager.

———○———

1

'Neath Shandon's Bells

Tim Cramer

With deep affection and recollection
I often think of those Shandon bells,
Whose sounds so wild would in days of childhood,
Fling round my cradle their magic spells.
On this I ponder where'er I wander,
And thus grow fonder, sweet Cork of thee,
With thy bells of Shandon, that sound so grand on
The pleasant waters of the River Lee.

THE 'PEPPER CANISTER' steeple of Shandon stands sentinel over Cork City. Houses, shops and pubs huddle together as if for protection below the limestone and red sandstone turret with its four-faced clock and famed bells. It is a cosy, if sometimes boisterous and deeply traditional urban environment, where in years gone by, neighbours would have tended to 'live in each other's pockets'. They would have known bustling Shandon Street as Mallow Lane, down which the farming folk of County Cork would have trundled their produce to the city markets, especially to the Butter Market which was nearby.

Into a sturdy house in this colourful area on August 15 1917, John Mary Lynch was born, known in the vernacular of this place simply as Jack, and destined for a record-making career on the sporting fields of Ireland.

The Lynch roots, like the roots of many other neighbours, were far removed from the city. They came from a small farm in Baurgorm, a townland east of Bantry. Jack's father, Dan, came to Cork at the turn of the century. He worked as an apprentice tailor at the firm of Daniels, Merchant Tailors, on the Grand Parade, and later at Cash & Co., Patrick Street.

Jack's mother was Nora O'Donoghue, whose family came from a farm near Glounthaune in East Cork, but like the Lynchs moved to the city. Nora's father was in the licensed trade and had a well-known hostelry, 'The Cork Arms' in MacCurtain Street. He also operated as a 'Broker' who regulated the price of corn each morning at the Corn Exchange. Nora also worked in Daniels as a seamstress. A few days after Dan Lynch's arrival at Daniels, her sister and fellow-worker came to her, full of excitement and whispered, 'Nora, come upstairs, a country boy has started work.' Romance blossomed, and in 1908 Dan and Nora were married.

In time, the Lynch family numbered nine. Timothy, or 'Theo' as he was known, became a teacher and was an officer of Glen Rovers Hurling Club for over 20 years. Charlie joined the Priesthood and Finbarr became a Senior Civil Servant. All were outstanding hurlers and figured very prominently with the Glen for many years. Another brother, Jimmy, died when he was just two years old. The two girls worked in Cork City, Eva with the Irish Dunlop Company and Rena with Browne & Nolan booksellers.

Jack and his mother.

The youngest, Jack, was the wild one of the family and was always the leader of the pack when any devilment was being organised. In later years he described his father as strict but fair, a tall, dignified-looking man, quiet and modest in all things. He had played

Gaelic football in West Cork, and in the city with Nils, a team linked to the drapery trade. He was an accomplished bowl player and had an interest in all sports.

Their house under the shadow of Shandon Bells was nicknamed 'Grand Central Station' by the boys because of the frequent influx of country cousins on visits to the city. These visitors rarely got a good night's sleep because Shandon's Clock loudly marked every quarter hour. The locals, of course, were totally immune to this nightly music.

Jack and Finbarr went to school together for the first time in 1922, to St Vincent's Convent in Peacock Lane. Thinking that school was finished at the lunch-break at 12.30pm on their first day, they both ran home in the pouring rain to their surprised mother who let them know that they should have stayed until 3.00pm. They returned the next morning a little wiser. Three years were spent with the nuns and then both went on to the North Monastery, known locally as the North Mon.

Early school days at St Vincent's Convent.

Jack spent 11 years with the Christian Brothers, who, he said 'had a profound effect' on him. Academically, he did very well and gained a scholarship to the secondary school. In October 1932, whilst his academic and sporting careers were blossoming, a tragedy occurred, devastating the family and leaving the teenage Jack shattered. His mother died unexpectedly at the age of 48. She had gone into hospital, the nearby North Infirmary, for what was thought to be a minor ailment and was due to come home two weeks later. Jack and Finbarr were alone in the house when a nurse rushed up from the hospital to tell them that their mother had died. Fifteen-year-old Jack went to the hospital to confirm the worst, while Finbarr had the harrowing task of telling his father. Later, Jack was to recall, 'I walked around the streets for hours in a daze, and for years later I was deeply affected by the loss'. Mrs Lynch had been a very quiet, fastidious person, and Jack was very close to her. 'My mother's training as a seamstress made her fussy about our clothes and appearance. We were always well dressed, even if our clothes were usually hand-me-downs.'

A break in training, Glengarriff, August 1943.

Jack meets Máirín for the first time. (L to R) *Frank Casey, Jack Lynch, Noreen Dillon, Beryl Fagan, Con Prior, Máirín O'Connor, Finbarr Lynch, Sheila Crowley, Paddy O'Donovan.*

Following their mother's death, the Lynchs went to live with Nora's sister, Aunt Statia, and the O'Reilly family. They had a house at Vernon View on the South Douglas Road for six months, but the lure of the Northside brought them to 'Clonard' on Redemption Road. It was a crowded house with eight O'Reillys and seven Lynchs, though as time passed, the older Lynchs moved on. Gretta O'Reilly, Jack's first cousin, and her husband Tom Drummond, still live at this house, over 60 years since the families originally took up residence.

Acrobatics – Crosshaven, County Cork.

Jack does a balancing act with the help of Paddy O'Donovan.

Called to the Bar, 1945.

Front row: *Máirín, Jack, Mrs Hoeing, Mrs Finbarr Lynch.*
Back row: *Mrs O'Connor, Beryl Smith, Fr Charlie Lynch, Finbarr Lynch.*

Wedding day – August 10 1946.

On many occasions, Jack recalled with affection the outstanding North Mon teachers who prepared him so well for his career as a lawyer and a politician, despite his preoccupation with the many sports in which he was involved. Following his Leaving Certificate he sat a number of other exams, and secured a temporary position with the Dublin Milk Board. He joined the Civil Service in November 1936 and on December 29 was transferred to Cork and allowed sit as assistant to the County Registrar. Having taken an interest in legal affairs, he decided to study law and commenced a part-time course at UCC in 1941. This took two years and the final two years had to be spent at Kings Inns in Dublin. He transferred to the Department of Justice in Dublin and completed his studies.

A holiday in Glengarriff in 1943 led to a meeting with a group of girls including a young lady, Máirín O'Connor. They were married on August 10 1946, and Máirín, herself a sportswoman (she played hockey and golf), was to remain Jack's most loyal supporter throughout his life.

2

Scoring Goals at the Butter Market

A Personal Reminiscence

Finbarr Lynch

WHEN SCHOOL WAS finished, we used to rush home, throw in our school bags and grab our hurleys. We were always playing hurling, and when the evenings got too dark to see the sliotar or tennis ball, we turned to football. The only football available belonged to the Munster Football Association, which we borrowed from our uncle, Mick Donoghue, who was chairman of the MFA at the time. The pillars of the Butter Market served as our goalposts and many outstanding goals and brilliant saves were witnessed daily. As there was scarcely any traffic on the streets, the biggest problem we had was to keep an eye out for the Gardaí as it was against the law to play ball on the streets. Once they appeared, we generally made good our escape through the maze of streets and laneways. Jack was always first away, but I can recall him trying to scramble over a wall when a Garda caught him by the coat. Jack decided to cut his losses, and leaving the coat with the Garda, made a quick getaway.

We had our own companions including Paddy O'Donovan, Frank Casey, Mick Twomey and the famous Buckley brothers. Also in the group were Eugene Noonan and his brother Ritchie, Jack Cullinane and Johnny Mahony. The Noonan brothers both played together for the League of Ireland soccer team in the 1940s, and 'Blondie' Mahony played with Liverpool and Cork Bohemians at that time.

Hurleys were prized possessions and we used to buy 'shape-outs' from O'Connell's sawmills in Leitrim Street for a few pence and finish off our own hurleys. On wet days we played in the cellar of our house. The space was confined and the play was very tight. It was here that Jack developed the skill of controlling and getting the ball into his hand in a crowded area. Later on, during major games, I often witnessed him emerging from a ruck with the ball in his hand to the consternation of the opposition. The hurling in the cellar certainly paid dividends.

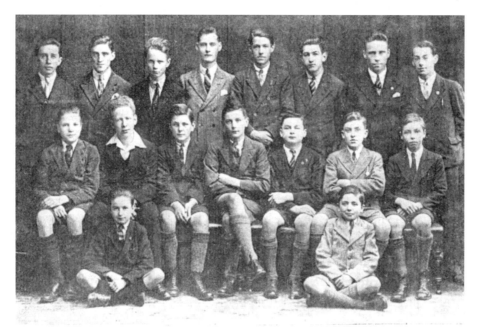

1931, primary scholarship holders and teachers.
Thirteen-year-old Jack Lynch is seated in the centre.

As we grew older, we moved up to the open spaces of the Fair Field where others joined us from the surrounding areas, many of whom later went on to achieve fame with Glen Rovers and Cork. Many thrilling games were played on the hard surface, and it was here that Jack further developed his hurling skills. When the games were over, we washed ourselves and drank water from the pump at 'Mickey' Sullivan's pub and made our way home in time for the tea and some homework for school the next day.

Jack was a natural left-handed player from the first day he caught a hurley, but on many evenings when we had finished our sessions, he would stay on by himself, just practising with his right hand. When he came to play competitive hurling, he was better with his right than with his left.

St Nicks North Parish U-16 football champions, 1929.

Front row: *J. Sheehan, P. Riordan.*

Second row: *J. O'Donoghue, John Lynch, C. Lynch, Jack Lynch, W. Luttrell.*

Third row: *T. O'Reilly, W. Corkery, L. O'Keefe, D. Byrne, M. O'Brien, T. Kiely, C. McGrath.*

Back row: *A. White, P. Corkery, T. McCarthy, F. Lynch.*

The Street Leagues of the late 1920s and early '30s were the only organised competitions available to us at that time. These contributed enormously to the development of the many great players who came out of the Blackpool/ Shandon Street area of the city. In 1927, Jack followed Theo, Charlie and myself to Glen Rovers. He immediately came under the influence of Paddy O'Connell who was in charge of the underage sections in the club, and who was to be Jack's guiding light for many years. Jack always remembered with affection, in the many articles he wrote, the special interest Paddy took in his progress. 'He taught me so much, resulting in me playing on the Glen and St Nicks Minor teams when I was 14'. Paddy O'Connell also took Jack on his first visit to Croke Park to witness the All-Ireland finals of 1931 against Kilkenny, which Cork won after the second replay.

In 1929 at the age of 12, Jack figured on the successful St Nicks Under-16 Juvenile Football team that won the North Parish Championship. Charlie and myself played on the same team. This was most unusual for three brothers to play on a winning Under-16 team.

He had many heroes, but 'Fox' Collins of his own club was his number one. The first Glen man to play in an All-Ireland Final, he was on the winning Cork teams of 1928, '29 and '31. Both of them played together on the winning Glen teams from 1934 to 1940 and the Cork teams from 1935 to 1938.

Jack possessed many outstanding attributes. He was physically big, and had amazing speed and strength, which gave him an enormous advantage, especially as a youngster. Before he was 18, he had figured on very successful North Mon, Glen Rovers and St Nicks teams. He also played on both Cork minor hurling and football teams, was very successful in school athletics and swimming competitions, and also played handball. He was a marvellous reader of a game and had total recall of everything that occurred during a match, with the ability to analyse every part of the action. He made hurling appear a simple game and this apparently easy expertise was not always fully recognised. His free-taking was a feature of his game, especially long-distance efforts. Jack was always very tense before a big game: his face would be drawn and he would be very nervous. All this disappeared once the match began. He gave the impression of always being in charge of events on the field and I am told that he was the last Cork hurler to make changes and generally direct operations while playing. He never resorted to unfair tactics of any kind and was never warned during his long career, though he was well able to look after himself when the occasion arose. Football always came second to hurling, but when Jack went to Dublin and played with the Civil Service in 1944-45, it greatly improved his ability and confidence and he went on to win a football All-Ireland medal in 1945.

**Jack Lynch with the 1930 Glen Rovers team
defeated by Blackrock in their first senior final.**

Front row: *J. Lynch, P. O'Connell, J. Burke, P. Collins (Capt.), J. Leahy, W. Deasy, D. Cremin.*

Back row: *C. O'Keefe, D.M. Dorgan, J. O'Leary, W. Hyland, C. Sheehan, J. Corkery, P.J. Dorgan, J. Lee, D. Daly.*

He was a very strong opponent of the 'ban' on GAA players playing rugby and soccer, and felt it had no place in the Association's rules. He refused to attend the presentation of Munster Championship medals to the winning Cork team of 1939, as Jim Young, one of his Glen Rovers' team-mates was not allowed attend, having been suspended for attending a rugby dance. Paddy O'Donovan and himself were both suspended in 1946 for attending a final Irish rugby trial in which his brother-in-law, John Harvey, was playing. He also strongly opposed the 'ban' on Gaelic games in many well-known schools and colleges run by religious orders.

When he retired from playing, he regularly attended club and county matches. He made great friends, especially with opponents from his own era. He was a great admirer of Mick Mackey and they had many tussles on the field but remained firm friends. He used to say that he never saw a goalkeeper to compare with Paddy Scanlan, the Limerick keeper of the '30s and '40s, and he had great admiration for Paddy Phelan and Jimmy Langton of Kilkenny. He always reckoned that John Keane and Christy Moylan of Waterford were amongst his most skilful and outstanding opponents but he was unceasing in his admiration of, and praise for, Christy Ring. He always felt that Christy was a man apart.

Jack with John Keane at the 1966 Munster final.

3

The Underage Years

IN THE 1930s, organised GAA activity was confined to the minor grade (Under-18) and the various competitions in the schools and colleges. In Cork City, the north and south areas organised their own parish championships and leagues mainly for Under-16 players. In 1929, St Nicks won the football championship and Jack Lynch played on this team with his brothers, Charlie and Finbarr. Glen Rovers won the 1930 hurling competition and Jack and Finbarr were again on the winning team, but it was in the minor grade that Jack stood out. In 1930, at the age of 13, he figured on the St Nicks' team which lost the minor county final to Macroom. Success came in 1932 and '33 and Jack figured prominently in those victories. The footballers reached the county final again in 1935 only to lose once more to Macroom. Glen Rovers had outstanding minor hurling teams throughout the 1930s and reached the county final six years in a row, from 1932-37, winning four titles. Jack captained the winning teams of 1933 and 1934.

On the inter-county scene, he played on the Cork hurling teams of 1933, '34 and '35 and the football teams of 1934 and '35 without success. Tipperary were the 'kings' of minor hurling and dominated this grade for many years. Jack often recalled that when Tipp. brought on subs during the game, every one of them seemed to be bigger and better than the player who was taken off. On the football scene, the Cork team lost to Kerry in 1934 and to Tipperary in 1935.

Paddy O'Connell with his 1932 minor team.

Front row: *D. Daly, J. Young, J. Lynch, P. Murphy, D. Geaney, C. Buckley, J. O'Donoghue.*

Back row: *W. Hyland, M. McGrath, D. Herlihy, C. Lynch, T. Kiely, L. O'Keefe, J. Leahy, M.J. O'Leary, D. Johnson, P. Barry, J.P. Long, P. O'Connell.*

1935 Cork minor team.

Front row: *D. Lynch, P. Riordan, J. Crowley.*

Centre row: *D. Creedon, P.J. Riordan, C. Atkinson, C. McCarthy, B. Culhane, T. Dorgan, D. O'Mahony, M. Goggin, W. Campbell.*

Back row: *D. Kiely, D. Andrews, M. Flynn, P. O'Callaghan, J. O'Reilly, D. Norris, C. Sweeney, D. Healy, W. Buckley, J. Quinn, J. Lynch (Capt.), D. Lynch, J.P. Creedon, J. Desmond.*

Glen Rovers Minor County Champions 1933–34.

Front row: *J. O'Leary, D. Creedon, W. O'Connor, J. Lynch (Capt.),*
Rev. Fr Barrett, T. Dorgan, D. Lynch.

Centre row: *T. O'Reilly, W. Hyland, P. Riordan, P. Callaghan, M. McGrath,*
P.J. Riordan, F. Herlihy, F. Forde, P. O'Connell, P. Murphy.

Back row: *P. O'Donovan, W. Goggin, R. Culhane, M. Goggin, C. Mulcahy,*
A. Mulcahy, P. Collins.

Jack Lynch's underage sporting career ended with great success in the club competitions, but disappointment with the inter-county results. He was to march on to further glory with North Mon where he played a leading role in their record-breaking achievements of 1934, '35 and '36.

4

Tar Barrels Blazed for the Winners

The North Mon Years

Paddy Deasy

THE HARTY CUP has a very special place in the life of the North Mon, a school steeped in the tradition of Gaelic games. It is the ambition of every pupil who can swing a camán to someday wear the school's famous blue and white jersey and win a Harty cup medal.

Jack Lynch was to achieve this ambition and he won three Harty medals in the Mon's glorious run of four-in-a-row victories from 1934 to 1937.

In a special interview for the 1984 *Cork Holly Bough*, he recalled those fantastic victories that played a vital role in his hurling career:

> Nobody who lived through them can ever forget the excitement of those Mon-Rockwell finals at Mitchelstown. First the train journey, then the rival throngs on the streets – but with no damage, no vandalism, no violence – and then the great pre-match parade from the John Mandeville statue in the square to the playing field.

1934

Frenzied Excitement at Mitchelstown

In 1934, the golden jubilee year of the GAA, the Mon won the first of an historic four-in-a-row Hartys, defeating Rockwell College in a replay at Mitchelstown, amid scenes of frenzied excitement. The first game, also played at Mitchelstown, ended in a draw on the score: Rockwell 4-2, North Mon 4-2. The replay was played on Thursday April 26. Although it was a weekday afternoon, almost all businesses in the town closed down and the two town bands played the rival groups of supporters in procession from the town to the playing field. Two special trains had brought more than 1,500 supporters from Cork.

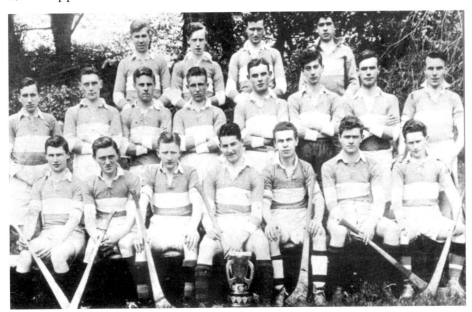

Harty Cup winners, 1934.

Front row: *C. Young, A. White, P. O'Donovan, D. O'Riordan (Capt.), D. Cusack, J. O'Driscoll, D. Scully.*

Centre row: *F. Lynch, J. Lynch, C. Buckley, M. McGrath, T. O'Riordan, P. Dwyer, J. O'Connor, D.J. Murphy.*

Back row: *P.J. Riordan, D. Moylan, M. Crockett, P. Callaghan.*

An exceptionally fine game wound up in favour of North Monastery by 7-1 to 3-3. Jack played at centre half-back. In the reporting style of the day, very few names were mentioned, but the reporter did enthuse sufficiently to say, 'Lynch was a strong opponent and created some good openings for the Mon'. Jack's brother, Finbarr, played right half-forward on the team.

A few days later on April 29, Jack played at left half-back on the Munster team that lost to Leinster in the All-Ireland Colleges inter-provincial hurling final at Nowlan Park, Kilkenny.

1935

Repeat at Mitchelstown

The same teams contested the 1935 Harty final which was played once again at Mitchelstown on Wednesday, May 8. There was a great attendance and two special trains brought the youthful supporters from Cork. Business was suspended in the town for the afternoon. In an exciting game the Mon ran out winners on the score: North Monastery 4-8, Rockwell 3-2.

The Cork Examiner reported: 'J. Lynch at right half-back was prominent all through, scoring long-distance points and, from his stirring play, set up the movements for the Mon goals'.

The victors received a wonderful welcome on their return at the Glanmire Railway station. A great crowd met them and headed by the Butter Exchange band and the Volunteer Pipers band, they paraded through the streets.

In the 1930s, Rockwell was one of the leading hurling colleges in the country and provided some of the most outstanding hurlers of that era. It also produced some brilliant rugby teams. In the 1935 final, Jack was marking the youthful Tony Brennan of Rockwell. Fifteen years later when Jack played his very last senior hurling championship game with Cork against Tipperary in Killarney, he again marked Tony Brennan, a great Tipperary hurler who later lost his life in a tragic accident.

Harty Cup winners, 1935.

Front row: F. Herlihy, A. White, C. Young, P. J. Riordan, C. Buckley (Capt.), M. Goggin, M. Kidney, P. Callaghan, F. Holly.

Back row: S. Daly, P. Riordan, J. Lynch, T. Riordan, E. Long, D. Doyle, C. McSweeney, J. O'Reilly, D. Moylan, F. Casey.

1936

The Final: Classic Encounter at Fermoy

While the Mitchelstown games dominated the most memorable games of the mid-1930s, the 1936 final was a classic encounter with great opposition from Coláiste Na Mumhan, Mallow. This particular year saw Jack captain the team from his position at centre half-back. Coláiste Na Mumhan was a teacher training college which had pupils from all the neighbouring counties. The game was played in Fermoy on St Patrick's Day, Tuesday, March 17. Again, special trains brought the Mon boys from Cork. This was the only time that the Mon and Coláiste Na Mumhan met in the final. After an epic battle, the Mon won in a thrilling finish on the score North Monastery 4-3, Coláiste Na Mumhan 2-6.

Harty Cup winners, 1936.

Front row: *M. Goggin, P. Riordan, J. O'Reilly, J. Lynch (Capt.), P.J. Riordan, P. Callaghan, M. Kidney.*

Centre row: *D. O'Kelly, M. Flynn, P. Hogan, C. O'Leary, S. O'Leary.*

Back row: *M. Cleary, L. O'Neill, C. McMahon, T. Winning.*

In *The Cork Examiner* report, Lynch heads the list of Mon players who contributed most to the win.

John Lyons, Cork's full back on the All-Ireland winning teams of 1952,'53 and '54, playing colleague of Jack's with Glen Rovers and St Nicks, and holder of three Harty cup medals in 1941,'42 and '43, turns back the years:

> I vividly remember the excitement which led up to the Harty finals in which Jack Lynch was involved, but especially the 1936 one when he was captain. The Mon played Coláiste Na Mumhan

in Fermoy. Brother McConville used to come around to the classroom selling the train tickets, which cost two shillings. We all prepared our blue and white colours and set off with our sandwiches ready.

The Mon won the game and Jack Lynch stepped up to receive the 'Harty'. He was our hero at that time and we all returned home happy and looked forward to the victory parade from the station to the school. Three bands were there to greet the team and thousands lined the streets. Up MacCurtain Street, down 'Pana', up the North Main Street and Shandon Street. Molly Owens, a Shandon Street trader, set the tar barrels blazing one at the top of Shandon Street and more at the school gate. The usual day off from school was granted after the team was introduced to the students in the school yard next morning, amidst scenes of great jubilation.

The Football Victories

An unexpected bonus was added to the Harty cup victories of 1934, '35 and '36. The Munster colleges football title was also captured, with many of the same players completing the double. On Saturday April 13 1935, one of the major shocks of the colleges' competitions occurred when the Mon beat Dingle CBS in the final on the score 2-5 to 1-5. North Mon led at half-time, 1-4 to 0-1. Jack Lynch played at full back on the Mon team which included many of his Blackpool team-mates. Included in what was regarded as an outstanding Dingle team was the rising Kerry star, Paddy 'Bán' Brosnan.

In 1936, the Mon proved that their 1935 victory was no 'flash in the pan' and went on to retain the title. Jack Lynch once more played a starring role in this campaign which ended with a win in the final against Ennis CBS on the score: Mon 0-5, Ennis 0-2. He scored two points in the match. By this victory he had achieved a remarkable record: three Harty cups and two football championship medals in three years, 1934, '35 and '36.

Munster Colleges football champions, 1935.

Front row: *D. Doyle, P. Riordan, M. Twomey, L. Murphy, F. Casey (Capt.), J. O'Reilly, J. Lynch, P. Callaghan, F. Holly.*

Back row: *F. Herlihy, D. Moylan, C. Buckley, P.J. Riordan, T. Riordan, E. Long, C. Young, S. O'Regan, J. Murphy.*

To be chosen on the Munster Colleges' inter-provincial teams was a major honour at that time. Jack was selected on the hurling team for three years, 1934, '35, '36 and on the football for two, 1935 and '36. The footballers were beaten both years, the captain in 1935 being the famous Kerry star of the 1940s, Paddy Kennedy. The hurlers were defeated by Leinster in 1934. Jack Lynch played at left half-back and at right full-back was John Keane, the outstanding Waterford hurler of the '40s. But success was not far away; the following year the province was victorious.

Munster 5–7 Leinster 4–4

The Cork Examiner reported: 'Munster defeated Leinster after a thrilling game at the UCC grounds. A stubborn Cork defence, in which Jack Lynch prominently figured, helped Munster to victory. The half-time score read Leinster 2-4, Munster 0-1.'

The *Irish Independent* reported that they were '... nine points down but still they won'. Included in the team were John Keane of Waterford and Tony Brennan, Tipperary full back of the '40s and '50s.

1936, Further Success: Munster 4–3 Leinster 3–5

'Munster win by a point in the Inter-Provincial colleges hurling at Nowlan Park, Kilkenny,' *The Cork Examiner* reported. 'It was one of the most thrilling matches of this series ever witnessed locally. The standard of hurling throughout would have done credit to a higher grade.' Jack Lynch played at right half-forward and captained the team.

Apart from his hurling and football successes, Jack also distinguished himself as an athlete, winning the Cork Colleges 120-yards hurdle title and took second place in the Munster Colleges 100-yards swimming championship.

The following was reported in *The Cork Examiner*:

> Cork County Secondary Schools and Colleges Sports under NACA rules were held yesterday at the UCC grounds.
> 120 Yds. Hurdles Final
> 1. S. O'Loinsigh (North Mon);
> 2. T. O'Laoctha (St Colman's, Fermoy)
> Time: 16.6 secs
> (Thursday 14 May 1936)

Jack Lynch's sporting achievements at the North Mon have never been surpassed. They place him among the elite of school and college athletes of his or any other era.

The North Mon has the unique distinction of providing the captains of five Cork All-Ireland winning teams:

Connie Buckley (1941), Jack Lynch (1942), Mick Kennefick (1943), Pat Barry (1952) and Tomás Mulcahy (1990).

5
Mol an Óige

Seo aiste a scríobh Jack Lynch i 1984 do
Sárchluichí le Sárimreoirí **le Pádraic Ó Gaora**

'Dé Domhnaigh, 24 Feabhra, 1962, i reilig Dhún Bolg taobh le Carraig na bhFear, i gContae Chorcaí, nochtadh leacht os cionn uaigh Phádraig Uí Chonaill. Seaniománaí ba ea Pádraig agus tugadh 'Athair an Ghleanna' air. Fuair sé bás bliain roimhe sin. Níorbh iad a sheanchairde i bhfoireann Glen Rovers amháin a bhí páirteach sa chuimhneachán sin ach ionadaithe ó chlubanna ar fud an chontae agus an chúige, agus bhí Ardrúnaí Chumann Lúthchleas Gael, Pádraig Ó Caoimh, i láthair chomh maith. Níor shároimánaí é Pádraig in aon chor, ná ní raibh mórán de mhaoin an tsaoil aige ach chomh beag. Cad ina thaobh a dtabharfaí onóir mar sin do ghnáthdhuine mar é?

Is é an fáth é ná gur chaith sé a shaol go léir ag cothú lúthchleasa Gael, agus an iománaíocht ach go háirithe. Níor chuir sé roimhe clú agus cáil a bhaint amach dó féin. Ní raibh uaidh ach ceardaíocht na hiománaíochta a mhúineadh don aos óg agus grá a chothú ina gcroíthe don chluiche.

Fiú nuair a bhí Pádraig ina bhall d'fhoireann sinsear Glen Rovers, b'fhearr leis a chuid cleachtadh a dhéanamh i dteannta na n-óganach. Nuair a bhí a laethanta imeartha thart níor bhac sé leis na sinsir a thuilleadh ach 'mhair' sé i measc na n-óganách, á dtraenáil, á dtreorú agus á spreagadh.

Cé gur aithin Pádraig Ó Conaill sárghaisce, ní dhearna sé a mhór de dhuine amháin ná a bheag de dhuine eile. Ní bhíodh sé ag súil ach le hiarracht mhacánta agus thugadh sé moladh nó dhéanadh sé cáineadh de réir mar a bhíodh sé tuillte.

Ar na saolta seo, sílim go dtugtar an iomarca aitheantais do na 'stars'. Na saoithe nó na nuachtóirí spóirt is mó is cúis leis an scéal seo. Ní thugann siad dóthain airde ar ghnáthbhaill na bhfoirne a thuilleadh, agus creidim go bhfuil drochthionchar ag an mbéas seo ar na foirne agus ar an spórt i gcoitinne.

Is cóir agus is ceart aitheantas a thabhairt don sáriománaí nó don sárpheileadóir agus an moladh a bheadh tuillte aige a thabhairt dó ach is é aimhleas na foirne a dhéantar má dhearmadtar gur ball d'fhoireann é. Foireann ar bith a bhfuil 'star' nó dhó uirthi buann sí cluichí anois agus arís – ach is í an fhoireann a bhfuil spiorad, compánachas, comrádaíocht agus comhar i measc a ball is minice a bhuann na comórtais móra.

Chun an comhar a spreagadh go héifeachtúil ní mór tosú ar an obair i measc na mionúr agus a thúisce a dhéantar é is ea is fearr. Ní mór a chur ina luí orthu go bhfuil cleachtach na himeartha go fíorthábhachtach agus go bhfuil an cleactadh sin riachtanach ní hé amháin roimh imirt cluichí móra ach an t-am ar fad.

Le linn an cleachtaidh caithfear aird na n-óganach a dhíriú ar ghnéithe imeartha ina mbíonn siad lag. I gcúrsaí iománaíochta, mar shampla, tá sé tábhachtach go mbeidís ábalta an sliotar a bhualadh os a gcionn san aer agus í ar eitilt, go mbeidis ábalta tarraingt uirthi ar an talamh agus go mbeidis ábalta í a bhualadh deiseal nó tuathal.

Ní hí forbairt na hiománaíochta ná na himeartha amháin is cúram don té a mbíonn freagracht na n-óganach air. Gnó leanúnach is ea é agus nuair a bhíonn an seisiún traenála thart ní mór na hóganaigh a bhailiú le chéile sa chlubtheach, i halla an pharóiste nó cibé halla atá faoi réir ag imreoirí an lae inniu. Is mó imeacht is féidir a úsáid chun na malraigh a choimeád le chéile, le spiorad a chothú iontu agus a misneach a mhúscailt.

Is mar sin a chaitheadh Pádraig Ó Conaill a shaol, ag fónamh do na hóganaigh go léir a raibh baint aige leo. Lena linn bhain Glen Rovers 18 craobh sinsear chontae ó 1934 anall agus bhain siad an chraobh sin arís i 1962, bliain a bháis, gan trácht ar na craobhacha mionúr, sóisear, srl. a bhain siad.

Tá seanfhocal sa Bhéarla a bhaineann le pinginí agus puint. B'shin í fealsúnacht Phádraig Uí Chonaill i dtaca le hiománaithe – "Tabhair aire do na mionúir agus tabharfaidh na sinsir aire dóibh féin".'

6

Cork's Little All-Irelands

The Cork Senior Hurling Championships, 1934-1950

Jim O'Sullivan

I T IS OFTEN referred to as 'The Little All-Ireland', such is the prestige of the Cork county senior hurling championship which has consistently attracted followers of the game from different parts of the country over the years. In keeping with the status of the county in the hurling world, it produced some legendary contests and consolidated the reputations of players who subsequently paraded their skills on the national stage. Fittingly, attendances reflected the status of the competition, reaching a peak in 1977 with a figure of 34,000 for the meeting of Glen Rovers and St Finbarrs in the final.

The proud history of Glen Rovers stems, in the main, from their extraordinary feat of winning eight titles in a row, starting in 1934. The name of Christy Ring is synonymous with the club though his career was only beginning when 'the Glen' won the last of those eight titles in 1941. By then, a host of players had become household names inside and outside the county – people like Paddy 'Fox' Collins, 'Josa' Lee, Jim Young, the Buckley brothers and 'Cooper' Moylan.

Jack Lynch was another who wore the colours of Glen Rovers and St Nicholas with distinction, and enjoyed parallel success at inter-county and provincial level. In time, the respect he earned as a player and a person would win him affection and esteem in his political career across all the parties.

1934, County Champions for the first time.

Front row: B. Barrett, P. Murphy, W. O'Connor, J. Lee (Capt.), Rev. Fr Barrett, J. Corkery, W. O'Driscoll, P. O'Connell.

Second row: A. Mulcahy, D. Moylan, M. Casey, M.J. O'Leary, T. Lynch, J. Burke, C. Buckley, P. Collins.

Third row: P.J. Dorgan, J. Lynch, E. Carroll, T. Kiely, D. Cronin, W. Hyland, D.M. Dorgan, P. Dowling.

Back row: T. O'Reilly, J. Foley, J. Leahy, J. Sheehan, J.J. Forde.

Joining senior ranks for the first time in 1926, Glen Rovers contested their first county final in 1930 when they lost to a star-studded Blackrock team. Four years later, the breakthrough came with the first of the record-breaking eight-in-a-row sequence. Careful nurturing of under-age talent, allied to the success gained by their players with the North Monastery in colleges' competition was to pay a rich dividend. In 1934, and still at school in the Mon, Jack Lynch played a part, albeit a minor one, in that initial county championship success. He lined out in the semi-final victory over the city divisional team, Seandún. It was a game, he was to say later, in which 'he didn't cover himself in glory'. He wasn't picked for the final against St Finbarrs but it was to bring him the first of 11 county medals. The same year, he won a second county minor hurling medal to add to the two minor football medals he had already won. With St Nicholas he was to gain further honours through the success of the intermediate team in 1937 and the seniors in the 1938 and 1941 football championships. In total, his career with Glen Rovers was to last 16 years, culminating in a victory over the 'Barrs' in the 1950 decider. It was to feature some memorable performances, one particular highlight being his display when he captained the team in the 1939 final against Blackrock, which had been billed as a game between the 'old' and the 'new'. The 1948 final is one that will always be recalled, because of the significant contribution he made to victory, again over Blackrock.

What was remarkable about his club career was the number and variety of positions in which he excelled – wing back, centre field and most of the forward positions. Again, while he won a second medal in 1935, he didn't play in that final either. In fact, there was no final played that year. The Glen qualified by beating Sarsfield's in the semi-final. Their opponents were to be Carrigtwohill. However, failing to have the game delayed on the grounds that a number of their players were injured, the East Cork team was ruled out of the competition.

Title number three was gained at the expense of Sarsfields in 1936, and the following year when the Glen won through to the final, their opponents were again Carrigtwohill. Not surprisingly, because of what happened previously, there was a lot at stake for the champions. In the circumstances they won easily, with Jack Lynch 'one of the younger brigade' of players who won praise for their performances.

Partnering 'Josa' Lee at midfield, he shared in the club's record-breaking achievement in the 1938 final against Midleton.

1939

THE CORK EXAMINER

ALL RECORDS BROKEN IN HURLING FINAL

Blackrock Crack Under Amazing Second-Half Victory Dash
Twenty Thousand Given Thrilling Game

Glen Rovers 5–4   **Blackrock 2–5**

Glen Rovers vs Blackrock the 1939 County final.

Jack Lynch leads out the Glen team in the St Nicks' colours.

The 1939 final with Blackrock was billed as 'the game of the century', a test of Glen Rovers' strength against the club which had annexed no fewer than 21 titles before the Glen made a breakthrough. Jack Lynch was captain for the first time.

At half-time in the game, Blackrock were in front by a point, 1-2 to 1-1, and they added a further goal and a point before the Glen were stung into action. Brothers Jack and Connie Buckley took control at midfield and Jack Lynch was highly influential after he was moved to centre forward, where Johnny Quirke had been dominant for the 'Rockies'. According to the match report 'he created havoc' amongst the backs. 'He rained ball after ball into the Blackrock goalmouth. Their players defended grimly but could not withstand the tremendous pressure,' it added.

1940

THE CORK EXAMINER

GLEN ROVERS MAKE IT SEVEN IN A ROW BY GREAT WIN OVER SARSFIELDS

Blackpool Hurlers Keep Secure Grip On Cork Hurling Title

Cork County final, Glen Rovers vs Sarsfields.

Jack Lynch leads his team including P. 'Fox' Collins, D. M. Dorgan, Jim Young, Dave Creedon, Dan Coughlan, Paddy Hogan and Jack Buckley.

Jack was captain again when Sarsfield's were beaten in a game remarkable for the scoring of 17 goals (10-6 to 7-5), with Charlie Tobin scoring six of the Glen's ten. In another context, P. 'Fox' Collins, affectionately remembered as the first of the Glen 'greats', bowed out.

1940 County Champions.

Front row: *D. Moylan, J. Young, D. Creedon, D. Coughlan, W. Hickey, J. Lynch (Capt.), J. Buckley.*

Back row: *P. O'Donovan, C. Tobin, P. Hogan, C. Buckley, P. Barry, D.M. Dorgan, P. Collins, D.J. Buckley, T. Murphy.*

1941

The Eighth In A Row

Glen Rovers 4–7   Ballincollig 2–2

The 1941 championship marked the last of the eight successes, representing an accomplishment that has never been equalled since. The title was won against Ballincollig, captained by another Cork great, Willie Murphy. It marked the retirement of many of the club stalwarts who had contributed so much to the record-breaking run, among them Connie Buckley who captained the 1940 team. The occasion was also noteworthy for another reason: a young player by the name of Christy Ring, playing at midfield, won his first county medal.

Glen Rovers team and supporters, 1941 County Champions.

The honour of being the team to knock Glen Rovers off their perch fell to Ballincollig in the 1942 semi-final, when Jack was captain. Ballincollig lost the final to St Finbarrs, who were again champions in 1943. One year later, the Glen were back on top, beating the Barrs with a team captained by Din Joe Buckley. Jack Lynch, now Dublin based, was a notable absentee and he was also missing when the club won their tenth title in 1945, against Carrigdhoun. Back in the team for the 1946 campaign, he was on the losing side against St Finbarrs in that year's final, and again the following year, in the semi-final against Sarsfields. However, three further medals were to be won over the next three seasons.

1948

Starting at left corner-forward in the 1948 final against Blackrock, Jack was to play a leading role after being moved to midfield – following the dismissal of Christy Ring. Blackrock also had a player sent off, but, in keeping with the traditions of the time, the match report did not name the two.

Jack Lynch was singled out for special praise in *The Cork Examiner* match report.

THE CORK EXAMINER

GLEN ROVERS REGAIN THE CORK HURLING TITLE IN HARD-FOUGHT THRILLING FINAL

Glen Rovers 5–7   **Blackrock 3–2**

Once again it was a real day out for the veterans. Jack Lynch's display was one that he must have seldom equalled in all his many Croke Park appearances. This player, who was a substitute on the 1934 Glen team which brought the title to Blackpool for the first time, won the plaudits of the crowd yesterday for his magnificent performance. He started at left corner-forward and before long he had shown a stylish touch by pointing from far out on the wing. It was when he moved to centre-field, however, that he really began to be the moving force behind the tactics which led to the Rovers' victory. He completely dominated play around midfield and he seemed to revel in the difficult ground conditions prevailing. As the game drew to a close he was as untiring in his efforts as at the beginning.

1949

1949 County Champions.

Front row: *D. Twomey, S. O'Brien, J. Hartnett, D. Creedon, D. O' Sullivan, D.J. Buckley, J. Young.*

Back row: *D. O'Donovan, J. Lynam, T. Logue, J. Lynch, P. O'Donovan, C. Ring, J. Lyons, C. O'Flaherty, M. O' Brien (Trainer).*

Title number 12 was gained at the expense of Imokilly in 1949 when he contributed 2-2. The first of his goals came in the nineteenth minute of the second half and it brought the Glen level. Another goal, from Christy Ring, gave the Glen the lead for the first time and the game was well and truly decided by the time Jack Lynch got his second goal near the end.

1950

THE CORK EXAMINER

GLEN ROVERS RETAIN COUNTY HURLING TITLE

Fieldcraft Proves Too Much For St Finbarrs

1950 County Champions.

Front row: *D. O'Sullivan, F. Corcoran, S. O'Brien, J. Lyons (Capt.), J. Hartnett, C. Ring, J. Nash, D. O'Brien.*

Back row: *M. O'Brien, D. Twomey, D. O'Donovan, D. Creedon, S. Daly, P. Hogan, C. O'Flaherty, P. O'Donovan, J. Lynch, V. Twomey, M. McInerney.*

Fittingly, Jack's career ended with another successful campaign in 1950, with a 2-8 to 0-5 victory over St Finbarrs. A point down at half-time, Seán O'Brien had the Glen on level terms from a 'seventy' soon after the resumption. Three other points quickly followed, with one in reply, before Jack got the first of their goals. 'A centre by Christy Ring, who was playing a great game, reached Jack Lynch and showing his usual cuteness, he eluded the defence to add an easy goal,' reported *The Cork Examiner*. It proved to be the turning point in the game.

Poignantly, the retirement of Jack Lynch subsequently severed the last links with the first winning team of 1934. He left behind him a legacy of memories for friend and foe alike, a lasting impression as a player of rare ability. Truly a giant among hurlers.

Seán O'Brien, captain of the Glen Team in 1951, wrote to Jack Lynch asking him to come out of retirement to play in the county semi-final against Blackrock. This letter was the reply he received.

UP THE GLEN
(Air: The Boys of Kilmichael)

The sun in the west it is sinking
And the long-thought-of battle is o'er,
The Barrs from the Dyke are retiring,
They'll boast of the County no more.
Hurra, for the gallant young Glen boys,
Those brave lads so plucky and true,
Who fought 'neath' the Green, Black and Yellow
And mustered the conquering 'Blues'.

We had Porter in goal like an eagle,
Paddy Hogan and 'Din Joe' so sure,
While that scion of Blackpool 'Jose' Looney
Showed for Sullivan he was the cure.
Dan Coughlan and Jim Young our wing halves
Are men without peer in the game,
While our Captain, Jack Lynch, in the centre
To the Glen has brought honour and fame.

Centre field it was manned by two stalwarts
Who can hold their own with the best,
Eamonn Young and Christy Ring they are famous
And have proved their worth in many a test.
Donie Twomey and Collins our wingers
In our victory had a big say,
They hurled in good old St Annes' style
And over much-boosted half-backs held sway.

Jack Buckley so fast and courageous
On the forty yards was a host on his own,
And his clever passes to team-mates
From the south side brought many a groan.
Our full forwards combined like clock work
Their approach work was graceful to watch,
And though the Barrs changed their backs and
their goalie,
Their bright stars met more than their match.

For Joe Kelly as fast as a greyhound,
And 'Cooper's' experience and skill,
Made nice openings for Charlie Tobin
And he found the net at his will.
We're proud of North Mon and Farranferris,
St Annes, Christy Ring and Blackpool,
And we know that the cup for the 'County'
Will find its way home again soon.

7

The Munster Hurling Championships

The heroic deeds on the playing fields of Munster during the championships of the 1930s and '40s have been passed on to us in newspaper reports, poems, songs and stories, bringing to life the atmosphere, colour and excitement of those marvellous encounters.

> There is more atmosphere in Thurles on the day of a Munster final than you will get anywhere else – even at Croke Park on All-Ireland days. Once you put your foot inside Liberty Square on the morning of the match until you leave in the evening, you will feel completely tied up in this hurling atmosphere. You breathe it in the very air of the place.
>
> *Paddy O'Donovan, Cork and Glen Rovers Star,*
> Clash of the Ash *(Raymond Smith)*

The intense rivalry between the competing counties has given the championship a special place in the GAA calendar. Games of frightening intensity are played at a furious pace with breathtaking saves, magnificent scores, heartbreaking misses and disallowed scores. Nail-biting finishes, last minute winning points, injury-time equalising goals give followers another day out. Forwards take on the goalie and backs, under dropping balls, and at times require treatment from the ever-present St John Ambulance crew for their efforts.

As a hurling man, a Munster man and one who took part in many a Munster hurling final, it is easy to go overboard when writing about that unique event in the sporting calender of Ireland. Not all Munster finals have been classics; in fact many times over the last thirty years or so Leinster senior hurling finals have surpassed their Munster counterparts as spectacles.

However, one cannot detract from the uniqueness of the Munster final, the quality of the hurling, the rivalry built up over a century, and the love of the game itself so evident in every one of the Munster counties, including Kerry.

Jack Lynch, Munster GAA Story, *1985.*

Jack Lynch played a major role in the Munster Championships from 1936 to 1950. Limerick were the dominant force in the 1930s, winning the title in 1933-35, '36 and '40. They were All-Ireland champions in 1934-36 and '40 and National League winners from 1933 to 1937. Mick Mackey was the hurling giant of the era, ably supported by his brother John and other outstanding team-mates including Paddy Scanlan, Timmy Ryan, Paddy Clohessy and Jackie Power. They defeated Cork in the earlier rounds in 1933, '34 and '35.

Jack made his championship debut against Clare in 1936, but Cork were defeated after a replay in atrocious weather conditions. He had played his first senior game with Cork against Limerick in the National League in 1935 while still at school. Tipperary ousted Cork in 1937 after a thrilling game on the score 4-3 to 3-5, and went on to win the All-Ireland. Cork had a dramatic victory over Limerick in the first round in 1938 and hopes were high for a major breakthrough but Waterford won the semi-final played in Dungarvan.

Better days were ahead. The war was coming but so also were the Cork hurlers. Stirring tussles with their Munster opponents, especially Limerick, were to bring major successes to the county. Jack Lynch captained the team in 1938, '39, '40 and '42. Despite severe travel restrictions from 1940 to 1945, thousands travelled by every conceivable mode of conveyance. The

1944 final became known as the 'Bicycle Final' when it was estimated that up to 25,000 supporters cycled to Thurles from all over Munster. The Cork fans free-wheeled all the way home, whistling.

1938

IRISH PRESS

CORK SHATTER LIMERICK CHAMPIONSHIP HOPES

Brilliant hurling in Munster Title shock

Cork 5–4   **Limerick 2–5**

Cork created one of the biggest sensations of recent years by defeating Limerick yesterday at Thurles in the first round of the Munster championship. The Leesiders, playing with wonderful dash and abandon, hit first time and hard right through an hour that was productive of a rare feast of hurling.

Limerick battled all they knew, and for long periods it was anybody's match. Tommy Kelly and Jack Lynch, however, proved the turning point as the Cork midfielders plied their front line with passes that Brennan, Moylan and Buckley pounced on to drive home scores that blasted Limerick's championship hopes.

'Green Flag'

Jack Lynch captained Cork and had his boyhood hero, club colleague and veteran of the Cork All-Ireland winning team of 1931, 'Fox' Collins, as a team-mate. Disappointment followed this outstanding victory and the team were well beaten by Waterford in the semi-final, 5-2 to 1-3. Waterford subsequently lost to Dublin in the All-Ireland final.

1939

IRISH INDEPENDENT

OVER 40,000 SPECTATORS AT MUNSTER HURLING FINAL

Youth and speed won for Cork

Scanlan saved Limerick from heavier defeat
Lynch shines in grand winning team

Cork 4–3   **Limerick 3–4**

Cork and Limerick compressed into one glorious hour everything that ever made southern camán clashes famous. It was a glorious, thrilling, all-exciting game, an event that set hearts throbbing madly and blood pulsating wildly. Class hurling at any time is the fastest ball game on earth. At Thurles yesterday, it was 'greased lightning' and of such play, adequate description is impossible. On the forty odd thousand that thronged Thurles, it left an indelible impression that can never be erased. Those not present can never get an adequate description.

Cork were the better team and they put great dash and fire in their play. To mention Campbell, Quirke and Young for a great half-back display is not to reflect on others of a sound defence. Lynch on the right wing, played one of his best games scoring one goal and two points.

It was a game that will live in memory, keenly but cleanly contested, the players showing a fine spirit. In all respects, it was another triumph for Munster hurling; and if a young Cork team is to be congratulated on a hard-earned victory, there is a tribute also due to Limerick who went down with colours flying, fighting every inch of the ground. They took their defeat like the good sportsmen and gaels they have proved themselves to be in the past. There were scenes of great rejoicing by Cork supporters at the end and a number of the Cork players were lifted shoulder-high and cheered loud and long.

Cork Senior Hurlers, 1939 Munster Champions.

Front row: *B. Thornhill, W. Campbell.*

Centre row: *P. O'Donovan, W. Murphy, J. Lynch (Capt.), B. Ryng, B. Dineen, T. O'Sullivan.*

Back row: *J. Buttimer, A. Lotty, J. Quirke, J. Barrett, J. Young, C. Buckley, M. Brennan, J. Barry (trainer).*

Jack Lynch captained the team to Cork's first Munster championship victory since 1931. He also captained the Cork football team which defeated Waterford 0-8 to 0-7, but lost in the Munster semi-final to Tipperary, 1-9 to 2-2.

1940

The 'Volcanic' Championship

All hurling followers looked forward to the 1940 championship and they were not to be disappointed. For excitement thrills, bone-crushing tackles, nail-biting finishes, pitch invasions, 1940 had them all. Cork had a thrilling win over Tipperary on the score 6-3 to 3-5, and defeated Clare by 7-6 to 3-5. Limerick and Waterford had to meet twice with the Shannonsiders winning the replay in the last seconds of the game. Hurling fever gripped the country.

Dick Stokes, a member of the winning 1940 All-Ireland team and one of Limerick's all-time greats recalls the 'Volcanic' Championship:

> I was fortunate to be a participant in the 1940 Munster finals between Cork and Limerick. Now, over 60 years on, I can still remember the tension and excitement of the games. Limerick had two matches against Waterford in the first round before scraping home. It was my first year and I looked forward to the final. I was playing with many very experienced players and we all seemed to knit together fairly well. Training and preparation for matches at inter-county level in those days was very different to what has been happening in recent years, both in length and intensity of training periods. Players at their peak were very fit, but then daily life was not dictated by the motor car – walking and the bicycle were the ordinary mode of transport. Special training for two or three weeks before a match was basically to top up the fitness of the individual and practise the skills of the game. As well as running and sprinting, hurling played a major role in training. Massage was also a major item. Our physical trainer, Martin Lawton, was an athlete in his younger days and then a very well-known dog trainer. He had a special mixture of olive oil, camphorated oil, a shot of whiskey and poteen (no doubt the dog rub) which when properly applied would stimulate any human being to greater things.
>
> Training usually finished on the Tuesday evening before the match with a 'get together' on Wednesday evening for a shower and a chat. There were no pre-match 'practises' or loosening-up exercises. Pulled muscles and other medical disabilities were very uncommon. The style of hurling in those days was also very different. The common features were overhead

striking with and against the ball, first time ground play with the ball 'doing the work', very much man-to-man play. Running with the ball on the hurley was not a feature, with very odd individual exceptions. Bunching was rare and four or five players trying to catch a falling ball in the hand would never occur. Hurleys were used with skill and accuracy – all features which made the game very exciting for the onlookers. This was the hurling that Jack Lynch grew up with and excelled at.

The team normally togged out in the hotel or other headquarters in the town and travelled by car to the field. The rise in excitement before the match was great with supporters in high mood. The entry to the pitch in Thurles for the players was through a narrow gate in front of the only stand; the crush could be great with the crowd high on excitement and anticipation. The Thurles stewards were noted for keeping 'law and order' amongst the spectators and it was not unusual to see an unruly man taken legs first, by three or four stewards and put inside the gate. There was no seating accommodation except for a few chairs inside the small entry gate for the Archbishop (a Limerick man at the time) and the President of the GAA or chairman of the Munster Council and a senior Tipperary County Board official.

Cork and Limerick had played the 1939 Munster Final. Cork were victorious by two points, had almost the same team in 1940 and so were regarded as favourites. Limerick had three or four newcomers on the team. There was more than normal competition between the sides and this, of course, spilled over to the spectators. The final would be the general topic of conversation at the crossroad for the weeks leading up to the match. The trains were still running even though the Second World War had started almost 12 months previously. All modes of transport including bicycles and horse-drawn vehicles would be put into operation. Those from a distance would often set out the evening before or very early on Sunday morning.

The pre-match atmosphere in the town and in the vicinity of the pitch was electric before the game with respective supporters displaying their badges, flags and other emblems. Three bands led the pre-match parade by the teams and the arrival of the team on the pitch was greeted with a roar from the crowd which continued throughout the match. Dan Ryan of Tralee was a most competent referee, fully in control of the job. Yellow and red cards did not exist. Thurles, the mecca of hurling, had a special atmosphere for hurling fans not found in other centres. Thirty thousand attended on this occasion.

The majority of the players on both sides were household names – about 12 were on the Munster Railway cup team that beat Leinster on the previous St Patrick's Day. Young lads playing hurling in the local field assumed the names of prominent hurlers in their practices.

The Munster final of 1940 relates to two matches – the first played on 28 July 1940 and the replay on the following Sunday, 4 August – both in Thurles and with the same referee.

Micheál Ó Hehir had begun his broadcasting career by then, usually in an open space on the sideline with little more than a microphone and a small table. He did an exceptional job and he added to the atmosphere of the occasion especially for those who were fortunate enough to have a radio, or be in easy reach of one.

THE CORK EXAMINER

CORK 3–6 LIMERICK 4–3

Another Cork–Limerick Epic

Cork level twice in desperate finish to hold Limerick
30,000 see glorious hurling in Munster Final

Last year's epic final at Thurles when Cork beat Limerick was equalled yesterday when the same counties again provided a breathtaking series of thrills in an hour of hectic hurling. The game this time was fought to a draw after Limerick had established what, at one time, looked a winning lead. Cork fought back in rousing style, however, and in a really great finish, twice levelled the scores so that they can meet again.

THE KERRYMAN

It was a game which was played at top speed. A game that at times resembled a battle of hurleys and in which every minute had its quota of thrills. The pace was indeed a cracker and in the hurly-burly of the play, it was surprising that injuries were not more frequent. The players fell to their work with reckless abandon. In many an attack the players went tumbling in bunches around the posts. The speed of the game never slackened. No sooner had a particular feat received its cheer than a counter blast roared its approval of another. No one could claim to have a surfeit of hurling such as was served up in this game. The speed of the game was another brand, speeding at times like greyhounds; the players took clash for clash, and sought more. If ash could sparkle, many a hurley would have burnt in this rare exhibition. Everywhere there was close tackling and fast striking with every inch of the ground tested and disputed. The accuracy of the deliveries was only equalled by the uncanny skill of the defence lines, and they had the busiest time of all.

Seamus Ó Ceallaigh

'Carbery' vividly described the match events in the *Cork Weekly Examiner*.

CORK WEEKLY EXAMINER

A MUNSTER FINAL

Thurles was no place for weak hearts in last Sunday's broiling heat and excitement. Every match between Cork and Limerick of recent years had its own individuality – fiercely earnest and packed with pulsating passages. Many of us thought the 1939 Munster final had reached hurling meridian. Best hurling game of the whole year it was. Yet this year's vivid memories switched 1939 to 'the limbo of forgotten things' and 'battles long ago'.

Scribblers are bankrupt of phrases. Our vocabulary is exhausted – we must invent a new language to describe modern hurling. And should we let ourselves 'go' we will be accused of 'bats in the belfry'. So overwhelming was that closing delirium of surging scores – like a crescendo of brass music – that 30,000 spectators were hushed and awe-struck – until cooling nut-brown draughts released the floodgates of admiring comment when impressed throngs once more trooped the ample square of Thurles. Good men and true that thirty: all in action to the stirring finish. Nineteen-forty was as like 1939 as two stacks of sound grain in adjoining harvest fields. But they were as different in flavour as wheat and oats: both wholesome; one richer than the other; last Sunday was the heart of the wheat.

Not so generous in yield perhaps – thirty thousand against forty-five reflected the feeling that Cork hurlers were improved and Limerick not quite so good. So we all thought. What guessers even the best of our hurling critics are. We might as well try to plumb mid-Atlantic with a fishing line as weigh the reserves of good hurlers on a great occasion. For hurling is largely a game of the spirit, though every nerve and sinew must be well strung and sweetly attuned to stand such concentrated and sustained tests as this hour's hurling brought. And there is more to come.

Thurles was just the same glad place of a thousand greetings. Championship hurling is a real bond between man and man. And there is a solid nobility of countenance about a hurling crowd unknown elsewhere. Old friends galore and all our cares forgot.

Hurling re-opened like rapier-play in a medieval battle. Limerick were racing like red deer on Knockfierna. Pat Clohessy was again a master of craft; the Mackeys were flashing in and out like spring salmon testing the rapids at John's Bridge at Garryowen.

They found a sluice and big Pat McMahon was through for a goal. Who said the Maigue estuary man was decadent? To prove his resurgence he crashed in under a grand Fedamore ball from one of Clohessy's longest flights – Buttimer again had no chance and the hemp squares bulged – Limerick seven points clear, and sailing home like winning oarsmen on a flood tide.

Few expected what happened. It was like the anti-climax in a Roman drama. Cork were still unconquered and undaunted. Like a good boat's crew they never lost 'form' under pressure. Buttimer and his backs opened up, and Cork's midfield – Barrett, Lynch and Connie Buckley struck out. Every man in Cork's fifteen rallied to the great demand. Campbell's rhythm of swing sent leather goalwards, and Ted O'Sullivan tore through for a goal. Four points behind.

Quirke made no mistake with a free. Three points behind. Then young fair-haired Stokes of Pallas flashed in, like a kingfisher on a stream, for a Limerick minor. Spectators were now throwing things about in their excitement. Youths roared approval; men swayed in the stands; colleens hid their heads lest a devastating score would swamp their brave hopes.

So the great game swung from end to end. Hardly was Stokes's point registered when Cork were surging inshore like a sudden summer hurricane from Inishclere. The Carbery man, Jim Young, playing a glorious game, was upfield and swung on a travelling ball. Deadly was his aim and perfect his timing – the ball sped in low trajectory to the netting. Cork a point behind!

Livid closing minutes like sunset in a lightning storm of vivid flashes and bombing clouds! Cork tearing in eager waves – Ted Sullivan and Brennan through the goal. A moment of doubt! Crossed flags. Score disallowed! Brief protest! On with the dance! John Quirke shaves the sticks. He makes amends. A placed ball would try most nerves. John is masterly in his precision – the ball sails for the levelling flag, and whistle. They meet again. Let us leave it at that. We to our memories and expectations of gold in store.

The Replay – August 4 1940

Dick Stokes takes up the story once more:

The trend of the drawn game gave rise to much discussion on the 'might have been', but the players and team mentors had to adjust to the job in hand – the replay on August 4. There was light training for a few evenings and much discussion on the plan of campaign. Many of the Limerick players were heroes of battles galore with experience in plenty of All-Ireland and Munster championship tussles. They gave valuable encouragement and advice to the younger players. There were no changes in personnel though some positional changes were made to strengthen what was perceived to be some weaknesses. The immediate preliminaries to the match were somewhat similar to the first meeting – the same tension and excitement amongst the followers.

Replays frequently do not come up to the standard of drawn games, but in this case, if anything, there was a distinct improvement. The pace was a cracker right from the start. Speed was the keynote with first-time striking and bouts of skilful overhead play which kept the crowd at fever pitch – one long thrilling thirty minutes of intense excitement. The marking was very close with very little room for fancy stick-work. Cork were in attack for most of the first half; balls were raining in on the Limerick defence. There were very limited opportunities for Limerick. At most, only four or five balls penetrated into the inner Limerick forward line. Limerick with their 'backs to the wall' put up a glorious defence which defied every move of the Cork forward line. This is reflected in the half-time score – Cork 0-3, Limerick 0-0. Surely, an extraordinary score for a hurling match played in perfect conditions of weather and sod. Turning over with a blank sheet things did not look good for Limerick. Yet Cork, who had most of the play in the first half had only one point from play and two from frees. During this period they had 13 wides against four for Limerick. On resuming, Limerick were on the attack and in a shock turnaround scored three goals and one point to the consternation of the Cork followers. Cork fought back and with ten minutes to go, were only two points behind: 3-3 to 2-4. All hell then broke loose. Hurling, the greatest game on earth, reached a peak point in excitement that years will not dim or distance sever from the recollection of the 25,000 that were thrilled beyond measure. The play swiftly moved from one end to the other, chances were gained and flitted away, reputations lost and won, new heroes applauded and the crowd swayed as never before. It was impossible for human beings to keep sane with full use of all their senses. Impossible to follow the play now with all depending on strokes that may go down in history. Both goals were in jeopardy every few seconds but defences held the day. With narrow shaves and brilliant goal-keeping by Scanlan, time raced fast – how fast few of the thousands present realised.

Cork were making desperate efforts to get the winning goal. In a sharp Cork assault on the Limerick goal, Micka Brennan was injured and removed from the scene on a stretcher. This incident added to the already angry mood of some of the Cork spectators who now moved on to the pitch. They covered most of the field but left the Limerick goal area clear. Appreciating the situation, one of the Limerick players smacked the ball over the sideline. By this time the 'sideliners' had mixed with the players. Play was suspended and it took about ten minutes for stewards and Gardaí to clear the pitch. At this stage there was only two or three minutes of play remaining. The sideline puck was only a foot or two wide of the Limerick goal. Then the Cork goal had a narrow escape.

In the last minute of play, the Rebel County had made a final bid to retain their crown, then slipping from their grasp. After a hectic tussle their skipper, Jack Lynch, got an open shot at Scanlan in the Limerick goal. The old reliable was equal to the last great test. He parried the shot and his clearance came to earth well out the field as the final whistle sounded to end the drama. During the last ten minutes of the match there was no score on either side, leaving Limerick winning by two points in a most dramatic game.

THE CORK EXAMINER

AMAZING SCENES MAR END OF SPECTACULAR CONTEST

Intense finish proves too exciting for crowd at Thurles

Limerick Take Championship Title From Cork By Two-point Margin

PITCH INVADED AT CRUCIAL POINT

Limerick 3–3   **Cork 2–4**

Were it not for the unfortunate series of incidents which took place in the closing stages of the game, the match would go down as one of the greatest, not only in the Munster championship, but of any championship. Anyone who was present during that last quarter of an hour had enough excitement to last a lifetime. It was an epic struggle par excellence, but the perfect finish was not to be – being almost virtually beyond the power of human nature to maintain that coolness that would have helped to bring about that fitting climax that could have been worthy of the glorious tradition of these two counties.

However, it is to the credit of the huge crowd, estimated at 25,000, that despite the invasion of the pitch, despite the intense excitement that prevailed, the pitch was cleared and the game was finished amidst excitement that really beggars the imagination for a description. At the time the stoppage occurred, lost time was being played and there were only two minutes to play. Those last two minutes proved a thrill a second and even in that period Cork went within an ace of snatching victory.

There was scarcely a minute to play and a goal in that time would have given Cork victory. The forwards worked like Trojans and when Jack Lynch got possession, the zenith of excitement appeared to be reached. Lynch, however, got little chance of steadying himself and though he made a gallant effort, his shot was just saved by Scanlan. The final whistle sounded immediately following the clearance.

Jack Lynch captained that team. His brother, Finbarr, recalls that he never saw him so disappointed after any defeat. He came home with some of the players in the back of a lorry which had travelled to the match carrying men and women from the Coal Quay, and they had a few drinks and a sing-song to ease the pain of defeat.

Mick Mackey later recalled, with pride, the 1940 finals:

Men like Dick Stokes, who made a world of difference, came along that season to our team. There will never be games, believe me, to equal these two games at Thurles in 1940. It was, you might say, the last year of the cars, for the restrictions on travel really began to bite in the succeeding seasons and yet they seemed to get there like pilgrims to Mecca. Nobody gave us a chance the first day, but we drew and beat them in the replay by two points.

Disappointment, however, was short-lived for Jack. Over the next ten years he went on to create extraordinary records which may never be equalled. He played hurling and football with club, county and province. He made himself available for challenge games, tournaments, leagues and championship. Whenever or wherever a match was played, Jack was there.

'A mighty team'. Limerick, 1940 All-Ireland Champions.

Front row: *P. Clohessy, M. Mackey, M. Kennedy, N. Chawke, R. Stokes, P. Cregan.*

Back row: *M. Hickey, J. McCarthy, T. Cooke, P. Scanlan, T. Herbert, J. Roche, P. McMahon, J. Mackey, P. Mackey, T. Ryan, D. Hurley, J. Power, M. Lawlor.*

Munster Championships, 1941–1944

1941

Major Disruption

There was a major disruption of the 1941 Munster championships due to serious outbreak of Foot and Mouth disease in Tipperary and South Leinster. Severe travel restrictions were put in place. Tipperary, who had defeated Waterford, were not allowed travel to play Cork in the semi-final. It was agreed that Limerick, who had beaten Clare, should play Cork and the winners would qualify for the All-Ireland final. It was also agreed that Tipperary would meet the winners of the Cork and Limerick match for the Munster Championship title when travel restrictions were removed.

Cork defeated Limerick on the score 8-10 to 3-2 and two weeks later became All-Ireland champions beating Dublin in the final 5-11 to 0-6.

Travel restrictions were lifted in mid-October and Cork and Tipperary met in Limerick on October 26.

IRISH INDEPENDENT

CHAMPIONS FALL TO TIPPERARY

Tipperary 5–4   **Cork 2–5**

Ten thousand spectators at Limerick yesterday witnessed one of the most thrilling Munster senior hurling championship finals ever played in which Tipperary spurred on by an early reverse, set about their task with zest and enthusiasm, which completely threw the champions out of their stride.

A feature of this game was that only three players from each side scored.

For Tipperary Bill O'Donnell, Jimmy Heaney and Tommy Treacy and for Cork Bobby Ryng, Jim Young and Jack Lynch who scored 1-4 of Cork's total. Connie Buckley captained the Cork Team.

1942

War-time travel restrictions had to be overcome but rival county supporters made their way to the various venues by every means available to them, long journeys by 'bike' being the most popular. Limerick had a close encounter with Waterford and qualified to meet Cork in one semi-final. The game was played in Limerick and provided another nail-biting finish. Limerick held the advantage for much of the game. Entering the last quarter, scores were level several times, but two late points gave Cork victory.

Tipperary defeated Clare in the second semi-final to qualify for a repeat of the 1941 final.

IRISH INDEPENDENT

MUNSTER HURLING CLASSIC

Cork Were Good Winners

Cork 4–15   **Tipperary 4–1**

Whatever doubts there may have been as to the best side in Munster in 1941, there was no doubt as to the better yesterday, for the All-Ireland champions were deserving winners. The pace of the Corkmen was the deciding factor in which their young forwards ran a grand Tipperary defence off their feet for 45 minutes and secured their reward in the last quarter.

A strong part of the team was the half-back line in which D.J. Buckley and Jim Young were outstanding, while Jack Lynch and Paddy O'Donovan had the better of a hard fought midfield tussle.

'Carbery' wrote:

Tipperary's strongest position on the field seemed to be at centre field. Willie O'Donnell and Jimmy Cooney, two six-foot men of the highest credentials, were in partnership, yet after ten minutes O'Donnell and Cooney were submerged by Jack Lynch and Paddy O'Donovan whose Glen Rovers teamship developed a dominance that threw Tipperary on their beam ends in the last quarter.

**Jack Lynch captained the Cork team who
went on to retain their All-Ireland title.**

1943

Waterford defeated Tipperary and Limerick beat Clare in the first round of the championship. Waterford created a shock by defeating Limerick in the semi-final by 3-7 to 4-3 and qualified to meet Cork who were victorious against Kerry in the second semi-final.

THE CORK EXAMINER

CORK COMPLETE THE DOUBLE

Waterford Made A Great Fight

Cork 2–13   Waterford 3–8

Following their victory in the Munster football championship final on the previous Sunday, Cork completed a fine double by taking the Munster senior hurling title when they beat Waterford at the Cork Athletic Grounds yesterday, 2-13 to 3-8, and qualified to meet Antrim in the All-Ireland final.

The fact that the lead changed hands five times and that there was never more than a major score between them showed that the teams were extremely well matched. Waterford led by 2-5 to 1-6 at half time.

John Keane at centre half-back had been dominating the game. On resuming, Cork made a number of changes, the principal one being moving Jack Lynch to mark John Keane. This made a major impact on the game and helped greatly to Cork's victory.

Mick Kennefick captained the Cork team and the attendance was 15,000. Jack Lynch completed the hurling and football championship double, as on the previous Sunday he had played on the Cork football team which won the Munster championship for the first time since 1928.

1944

IRISH INDEPENDENT

MICK MACKEY RALLIES LIMERICK TO FORCE DRAW WITH CORK

Cork 6–7   **Limerick 4–13**

Two goals down after five minutes and still six points in arrears coming to the last quarter, Limerick staged a magnificent rally at Thurles yesterday, took the lead with five minutes to go and eventually earned a replay with the holders, Cork, in the Munster hurling final.

Cork, who had defeated Tipperary in the semi-final, had a narrow escape after being well in command for most of the game.

This game was notable for outstanding displays by Mick Mackey for Limerick, and John Quirke for Cork, who scored three goals including a last minute one which restored Cork's lead. They were deprived of victory on the stroke of full time by a Dick Stokes' point.

Jack attends Fr Con Cottrell's ordination.

THE CORK EXAMINER

REPLAY

Hurling Replay Provides Another Thriller
Ring's wonder goal kept title in Cork

Cork 4–6   **Limerick 3–6**

In as sensational and dramatic a finish as ever graced a championship match, Cork All-Ireland champions beat Limerick in the replay of the Munster senior hurling championship final at Thurles yesterday by 4-6 to 3-6, the winning goal scored by Christy Ring about two minutes from the end.

Perhaps the greatest feature of all however, was the rattling fast pace set from the start. On the last occasion it was really only the last 25 minutes that produced the fireworks, but yesterday they had fireworks all the way, with Cork snatching the game out of a blazing fire in the closing minutes of the match.

With seven minutes remaining, Limerick led 3-6 to 2-5, but Cork refused to accept defeat. Morrison scored a goal and Quirke got the equalising point. It appeared that extra time would be needed but Christy Ring was about to unveil his talents.

IRISH INDEPENDENT

For those who were at Thurles, the last minute goal by Christy Ring which brought victory to Cork and defeat to Limerick, will remain a cherished memory of a wonderful artistic effort by a great hurler. To those who were not there, it will be recited for many a year to come, how the Glen Rovers man ran from his own half almost to the Limerick line with the ball bouncing merrily on his hurley, and then smacked it across for the goal that won the day.

It was a terrific match, hard, fast hurling and close scoring, which reached a crescendo in the closing stages when Cork put in their terrific finish. The midfield duel was keen and interesting. McCarthy and Lynch shone in the open play, but Cottrell was the soundest hurler of the four.

Both games attracted huge crowds despite severe travel restrictions. The games were known as 'the great bicycle finals'. Trains and buses were booked out. Every type of horse-drawn vehicle was put to use but it was the bicycle which took pride of place. Thousands arrived in the town on Saturday night, but the sight which was seen from dawn on Sunday morning was unbelievable. The roads into the town were jammed with cyclists coming from all over the province, many of them travelling over 80 miles to the final and back home again for work on Monday morning, sore but happy if they were from Cork.

Seán Condon of the 'Barrs' captained Cork to victory. Tipperary knocked Cork's four-in-a-row winning team out of the 1945 championship defeating them in the semi-final by 2-13 to 3-2. Tipperary went on to win the All-Ireland championship for the first time since 1937. However, Cork came back with a bang in 1946 defeating Clare 2-9 to 2-1 and Waterford 3-9 to 1-6 to qualify for the final against Limerick once more.

1946

THE CORK EXAMINER

CORK REGAINS MUNSTER TITLE

Cork 3–8   Limerick 1–3

In the presence of one of the largest and most enthusiastic crowds at a Munster final (39,000), Cork beat Limerick by 3-8 to 1-3. With hardships endured by thousands to get there, the pity was they did not see a more exciting game. However, there was no denying but that the better team won. Speed certainly carried the day.

1946 Cork team.

Front row: *C. Ring (Capt.), D.J. Buckley, P. Healy, W. Murphy, J. Kelly, T. Mulcahy, C. Cottrell.*

Back row: *J. Young, A. Lotty, M. Riordan, G. Riordan, C. Murphy, C. Murphy (Bride Rovers), P. O'Donovan, J. Lynch, J. Barry (trainer).*

There was very little spectacular hurling during the hour, which turned out to be a dour struggle. Goals by Joe Kelly, Mossie Riordan and Connie Murphy paved the way for Cork's victory, which was greatly helped by the supremacy of their midfielders, Jack Lynch and Con Cottrell. Christy Ring, who went on to lead Cork to another All-Ireland final, captained the team.

1946, Munster hurling final in Thurles, Cork vs Limerick.

1947

THE CORK EXAMINER

LIMERICK'S GREAT BID FAILS AT THURLES

A Game Of Thrills And Spills

Cork 2–6   **Limerick 2–3**

The match, despite the fact that there was a good deal of robust play, was generally regarded as the best Munster final since 1940. There was no denying the fact that the game was played in the best traditions of Munster hurling.

Relaxing at half-time, 1947.

Munster final, Cork vs Limerick. Jim Barry attends to Joe Kelly while
Gerry Riordan (14), Mossie Riordan (13), Con Murphy, D. J. Buckley, Seán
Condon and Jack Lynch.

IRISH INDEPENDENT

Limerick set the pace in the second half and what a pace it was.
Players stood shoulder to shoulder and swung, sometimes heedless or
unaware of where the ball went, and every break in play seemed to
come as a welcome relief. 'Such was the pressure on Cork that their
centre-field men, Jack Lynch and Con Cottrell became part of their
defence in a tremendous struggle to hold out the Limerick attacks.

A lecture by the referee to both teams at half-time seemed to benefit
Cork, for they showed renewed life, and their general play and level-
headedness kept them in front all the time.

1947, County football final. Jack followed by Dave Creedon.

Seán Condon once more captained Cork to a Munster championship victory.

1948

THE CORK EXAMINER

CORK SNATCH VICTORY IN CLOSING MINUTES OF THURLES THRILLER

Cork 5–3   **Limerick 2–5**

In the presence of the largest crowd (40,000) that human ingenuity could pack into Thurles sports field, Cork defeated Limerick. Some idea of the exciting finish will be gained from the fact that two of the winning goals were scored in the fifth and sixth minutes of the lost time period of seven minutes.

Limerick had slightly more of the play, then came a typical Cork raid. P. Collopy, the Limerick goalie fielded a hard shot and as he was being charged he tried to cut out towards the right wing. As he did so, Jack Lynch got his hurley to the ball and with a neat flick sent the ball to the net.

In the second half, the Cork backs covered themselves in glory and repulsed attack after attack. With injury time being played Cork led 3-3 to 2-5 and just before time ran out, Jack Lynch and Mossie Riordan scored a goal each to send Cork into the final.

The Final

This was Waterford's greatest day. Both of their victories were major shocks. So confident were the Cork supporters of victory that they stayed at home in great numbers. CIE cancelled two trains due to lack of interest and the attendance was estimated at 20,000.

THE CORK EXAMINER

WATERFORD'S SENSATIONAL DOUBLE IN THE MUNSTER HURLING FINALS
S.H. Waterford 4–7   Cork 3–9
M.H. Waterford 3–6   Tipperary 0–3

The Waterford team showed great speed all through the game and once they sensed that they were on the road to victory they played like a team inspired. Waterford had stolen a comfortable lead and they fought with grim determination to hold on to their advantage. There were moments when it looked as if the match would either end in a draw or that Cork would succeed in snatching victory, as it were, on the post and it was in the closing stages that the crowd got the full value for their money.

Waterford – shock winners, 1948.

Front row: *J. Goode, J. Cusack, A. Fleming, W. Galvin, J. O'Connor, V. Baston, C. Moylan.*

Back row: *J. Keane, E. Daly, M. Hickey, J. Ware, K. O'Connor, M. Hayes, E. Carew, T. Curran.*

Following the final whistle, Jim Ware, the Waterford captain was carried shoulder high to receive the cup. Waterford went on to complete a well-deserved senior and minor All-Ireland double and Cork won the National hurling league.

1949

IRISH INDEPENDENT

CORK'S UPHILL BATTLE TO FORCE DRAW WITH TIPPERARY

Dour Struggle For First Round Hurling Tie

Late Scores By Lynch And Murphy Give Leesiders Another Chance

Cork 3-10   **Tipperary 3-10**

An all-time record crowd for any first round match in the Munster hurling championship packed the Gaelic Grounds at Limerick yesterday. The attendance was 34,702, the gate receipts £3,498, a record. In all, the result was a fitting one and it will be a pleasure to see these thirty good men in action again. While the hurling was hard and fast from first to last, tempers were generally well under control, if one excepts a good exhibition of the 'old one two' by one of the players. The first half had some worthwhile passages, but it was in the second half that the crowd really got their money's worth as hurleys splintered in the stress of battle.

Tipperary looked set for victory after increasing their half-time lead of two points to four early in the second half, but Cork battled on. Jack Lynch, who had already scored five points, electrified the crowd.

The Cork Examiner described the closing action as follows:

Cork were still four points down with minutes to play. Lynch ran out almost to centre-field, gained possession of the ball and, showing a great turn of speed, brought it on his hurley past several backs and banged it into the net.

'...It took the old master, Jack Lynch, to display a real flash of his superb genius. Ranging upfield as the time was ebbing, he took the law into his own hands. Showing surprising speed, the ball in perfect hopping control, he bore his weaving way through the staggered Tipp. backs, and 15 yards out, he let fly with a short, sweet wrist-snap. The net bulged and Cork were one point behind.'

Carbery

The Cork supporters went wild with excitement. Then Bernie Murphy started on another solo run and sent over the equalising point. It was a great finish to a great game.

The *Irish Independent* also reported:

> Ring was always the danger man in the Cork attack, while B. Murphy and J. Lynch also earned the praises which Cork followers were singing as they left the ground. Lynch was in particularly deadly form, notching a goal and six points.

The replay was fixed for June 26 at Limerick.

The Replay

THE CORK EXAMINER

GRUELLING HOUR'S PLAY
IN BROILING SUNSHINE

Tipperary 2–8   **Cork 1–9**

After ninety minutes of hard robust hurling in which no quarter was given or asked, Tipperary defeated Cork in the replay of their first round tie in Limerick. At the end of normal time, the teams were level at 1-5 each and although the players gave every appearance of being exhausted after a gruelling hour's play in broiling sunshine, extra time had to be played as the winners must meet Clare on Sunday next.

1949 Tipperary team.

Front row: *P. Leahy, T. Ryan, M. Ryan, M. Byrne, P. Stakelum (Capt.), P. Caplis (Mascot), T. Doyle, J. Kennedy, J. Ryan.*

Back row: *P. Purcell, F. Coffey, S. Kenny, T. Reddan, P. Shanahan, J. Doyle, T. Dwyer, S. Maher, S. Bannon, T. Brennan, J.J. Callanan, G. Doyle.*

Cork were on top all through the hour and led with injury time being played by a goal. The crowds were leaving, but in the 64th minute, Jimmy Kennedy sent a lightning shot past Tom Mulcahy for the equalising goal.

Then came more drama. There was a long delay before both teams agreed to play extra time.

Pat Stakelum, the Tipperary captain recalls:

> Many of the players on both sides were so exhausted from the intense heat that they felt the game should be replayed again. Paddy Leahy, the Tipperary boss, was uncertain about what should be done when he heard the different views of his players. Jack Lynch came across the pitch and Paddy Leahy stopped him. 'What do ye think?' asked Paddy. 'I have enough of it,' said Jack. With that Paddy ordered his players into the dressing room. He stood up on the table and called for silence. 'If there's any player here, who does not want to play extra-time let him stand over to one side,' he shouted. No one moved and we prepared again for battle. In the meantime, the Cork team stayed out on the field which, I believe, was no great help to them. We lasted the pace better on the resumption, and a goal by Mick Ryan before the break set us up for victory. With time running out, Cork continued their pressure for an equalising goal but had to be satisfied with a point which brought an end to 150 minutes of a stirring Munster championship battle.

Tipperary went on to win the All-Ireland title for the first time since 1945.

1950

IRISH INDEPENDENT

TIPPERARY OUST CORK IN MUNSTER FINAL THRILLER

Tipperary 2–17   **Cork 3–11**

Action at the Munster Championship, 1950.

J. J. O'Brien (Cork) tussling with Mickey Byrne and Tony Brennan with Willie John Daly and Jack Lynch ready to pounce. The referee Bill O'Donoghue of Limerick seems to be awarding a free to Cork.

Tipperary defeated Limerick and Clare, and Cork beat Waterford to qualify for the final on July 23 at Killarney. The official attendance was returned at 39,000 but some gates were forced open and walls scaled, and it was reckoned that up to 50,000 were present.

The game was a thrilling exhibition and ended in a welter of excitement. Tipperary were in control for much of the match but Cork reduced their eight-point lead to three and were unlucky not to equalise.

The *Irish Independent* reported:

> From the first minute to the last, the exchanges were fast, fierce and skilful, but no matter how hard bodies or sticks clashed, there was never an unsporting incident to mar the hour. It was play which had a heart-throb per second for the rival supporters as each side in turn attacked and defended, as the occasion demanded. There was no denying that Tipperary deserved their success but Cork took a good share of the honours.

Stewarding arrangements broke down and ten minutes from the end the referee stopped the game for a considerable time.

Tipperary's centre half-back, Pat Stakelum, recalls:

> But for Jack Lynch, the match may never have finished. He went along the goal line appealing to the Cork supporters to get back and let the game go on. They responded to the appeal and moved back off the field. Having done that and after the resumption of the game, he proceeded to score a point with his boot, having lost his hurley. He had a point blank shot for a goal stopped by Tony Reddin and then scored Cork's third goal to keep the unbelievable excitement flowing. But time ran out and Tipperary went on to retain their All-Ireland title, defeating Kilkenny in the final.

This brought an end to Jack Lynch's Munster championship involvement which spanned from 1935 to 1950. He played in 15 Munster Senior Finals during these years:

Hurling: 1939, 1940, 1940 (Replay), 1941, 1942, 1943, 1944, 1944 (Replay), 1946, 1947, 1948, 1950.

Football: 1943, 1945, 1947.

8

Mackey – A Formidable Foe

A Tribute by Jack Lynch, from *The Mackey Story*
by Seamus Ó Ceallaigh and Seán Murphy

'On the field he was so formidable that one approached any possible encounter with him with trepidation. Off the field he was so easygoing, modest and friendly that one found difficulty in identifying the player on the pitch with the Mackey on the street. My encounters with Mick Mackey on and off the field were many but I will confine myself to recalling just a few of them. When I first came on to the Cork senior hurling team in the 1930s, Mick was already well established in hurling lore, having played in successive All-Ireland finals from 1933 to 1936, captaining Limerick to a smashing win over Kilkenny in 1936.

My first Munster championship game against Limerick was shortly after that. I played at left half-back and Mick, as usual, at centre half-forward. Following a tussle around midfield in which neither of us was involved, I kept watching what direction the ref. would point the free which ensued. Mick, apparently, having made up his mind that it would be against Cork, ran in towards our goal, without waiting for the referee's decision. As he passed me he gave me a hefty bump. Although it did not hurt I looked after him as he jogged on. I was quite annoyed, and he simply nodded, and smiled back at me over his right shoulder as if to say, "On occasions like this keep your eye on your opponents as well as on the ref." I frowned back at him as if to say, "Message received; lesson learned".

Glen vs Ahane, 1947, at UCC Grounds.

Donie Twomey and Mick Mackey tussle for possession as Glen players Seán McCarthy (Glen Rovers), Mossie Holly, Eamonn Young and Jack Lynch await the outcome.

A couple of years later, in one of those great tussles that Cork and Limerick had in the Munster championship in the late 1930s and early '40s, Mick and I were chasing a ball at full flight from about the same distance and from opposite directions. It was as if we came to an instant pact, 'ignore the ball and have a fair go'. We did – shoulder to shoulder – and we knocked each other flat. By the time we picked ourselves up the ball was at the other end of the field. That was that – no hard feelings but a few tender spots to take home.

The last time I met and spoke to him was at Christy Ring's funeral. I will always regret that I was unable to attend Mick's. On the morning of Mick's funeral I was about to leave our West Cork cottage to drive to Castleconnell when my wife suddenly remembered a last-minute message she wanted to give me. She dashed down the stairs, slipped and broke her elbow badly.

Fortunately, I heard her cry before I left, so instead of going to Castleconnell, I drove her to hospital.

A couple of years before Christy Ring's funeral, Mick and I attended the Hurler's Golfing Society outing at Thurles Golf Club – an activity for which Dermot Kelly works so assiduously. Mick and I were paired together though not in the competition proper. We played a few casual holes and for the first time in our 'golfing' careers, we attracted a gallery of about 20 people. My golf was atrocious! Mick's was a lot better, though without intending to be unkind, that doesn't say much. I said to Mick, "If we played as well as this in Semple Stadium 40 years ago, we wouldn't have attracted a gallery the size of this one." Mick's response was his characteristic sniff and wry smile.'

**Hurlers Golf Outing in September 1975.
Jack and Mick Mackey on the first tee.**

9

The Seven All-Ireland Hurling Finals

Donal Keenan

WITH THE IMPATIENCE typical of youth Jack Lynch wondered as the decade of the 1930s reached its end if he would ever gain the rewards he desired in hurling. Although he had only made his championship debut as a 19-year old in 1936 against Clare, by the time the championship of 1939 came around he was beginning to despair. He hadn't even played in an All-Ireland final then which greatly concerned him. 'There were many occasions when I thought I would never win an All-Ireland medal,' he would comment in later years.

The year 1939 was to be the turning point for Lynch and Cork. It was the start of an extraordinary chapter in the history of Gaelic games in general and hurling in particular. Over the next nine championships Lynch would play in seven All-Ireland hurling finals and win five, including an historic four in a row. He would also play in a football final and win, to put together a string of six successful appearances in All-Ireland finals, a record that has never been matched.

When Cork played Limerick in the Munster final in Thurles in 1939 they were seeking their first provincial success since 1931. Lynch was captain and a goal in the final minutes earned them the right to play in the All-Ireland final. Inevitably, Kilkenny became the opponents and the game went down in history as one of the greatest.

Two days before the final, on September, Germany invaded Poland, signalling the start of World War II. In Ireland, the battle for supremacy at Croke Park was foremost in the minds of the hurling public and the 39,302 who travelled for the first final meeting of the old rivals in eight years would not be disappointed.

The players and supporters awoke on Sunday morning to the sound of torrential rain. It continued to fall until the early afternoon but subsided just before the game started. In fact, there was bright sunshine to greet the teams as Lynch led out the Cork team which included some famous names like Buttimer, Lotty, Thornhill, Murphy, Quirke, Young and Dineen. Kilkenny had an equally illustrious line-up, including Phelan and Larkin from the 1931 team, as well as Langton, Leahy, Grace and Kelly.

All-Ireland final, 1939.

Jack Lynch and Jimmy Walsh lead the Cork and Kilkenny teams.

1939

IRISH INDEPENDENT

KILKENNY TRIUMPH IN HISTORIC FINAL
Kilkenny 2–7   Cork 3–3

Even with the benefit of the wind on their backs, a Cork team inexperienced at this level began slowly — the game was started with a throw-in by GAA President Paddy McNamee — and within three minutes were 1-1 to 0-0 behind; Jimmy Phelan scored the goal. Lynch opened the scoring for Cork but they were to struggle until half time when they trailed by 2-4 to 1-1.

The game had just restarted when the crowd and players were startled by a clap of thunder. It was a portent of things to come. What followed was a thunderstorm of extraordinary proportions with thunder and lightning accompanying a heavy downpour. So bad did conditions become that spectators could not make out the identity of some of the players, leading to confusion immediately afterwards over the identity of the Kilkenny player who scored the winning point.

The spectators sitting in the open had to seek refuge from the elements at stages during the second half. The journalists in the press box situated in the front row of the Cusack Stand tried to find alternative accommodation to allow them to take notes and remain dry. On the field a battle royal was taking place.

The Cork players had found their feet and mounted a spirited fight back. Lynch started with a goal though Kilkenny's Paddy Phelan played a huge part as he repelled wave after wave of Cork attacks. As the game reached its climax Willie Campbell drove a Cork free goalwards, it fell through a number of defenders and hurleys and ended in the net, Ted O'Sullivan possibly getting a touch to it on the way. There was just two minutes to go – time for plenty of excitement and a little controversy.

The newspapers the following day awarded the honour of scoring the winning point to Terry Leahy. It was, however, Jimmy Kelly who had gathered a free by Paddy Phelan and sent the ball over the bar from 25 yards.

The legend of this game grew and grew. One account of the winning score suggested that Kelly had feigned an injury and was seen by the Cork defence limping out from his position in the full forward line and bending down as if in pain. Then Phelan drove the ball towards Kelly and he miraculously recovered to take possession and score as the Cork defence believed he was out of the game.

Kilkenny All-Ireland Senior Hurling Champions, 1939.

Back row: *P. Blanchfield, P. Phelan, P. Grace, P. Larkin, T. Leahy, J. Walsh (Capt.), B. Burke, J. Kelly*

Centre row: *M. Dalton, J. O'Connell, J. Gargan, S. O'Brien, J. Phelan, B. Hinks, M. Oakes.*

Front row: *M. Power, J. Langton, J. Mulcahy.*

While the story has been repeated up to modern times, it has been denied by Kilkenny's Jimmy Phelan, the man who scored the two goals in the game. 'Kelly would never have done that,' he recalled much later. 'He was too much of a gentleman.' Phelan recalls that the ball was sent into the Hill 16 goal and broke just to the right of the uprights. Kelly pounced and took his score.

Kilkenny's Jim Langton later recalled the Campbell goal that levelled the game. 'It began to look like a draw and considering the appalling conditions under which the game had been played, probably all 30 players would have settled for a second meeting.'

Of Kelly's winning score, his recall was that the ball came off a weak clearance after a Phelan 'seventy'.

Phelan's description of the poor conditions and their effect gave a 'colourful' insight into the day. 'The dye on our jerseys ran into our togs,' he said.

It was a disappointing day for Lynch who missed a number of chances towards the end, but Cork were considered unlucky not to have got at least a draw, a fact remarked on by Lynch immediately after the game. 'We were under a handicap when Kilkenny got a flying start but we are entitled to credit for the great recovery we made under the terrible weather conditions throughout the last quarter.'

The Cork and Kilkenny players could not have known it at the time, but this game marked a dramatic change in fortunes for the counties. While Cork would go on to become one of the most successful teams in the history of hurling, Kilkenny would have to endure eight barren years, caused to a great extent by the foot and mouth epidemic which would restrict the opportunity for playing the game and caused the cancellation of club hurling for a year.

Following their defeat by Limerick in the 1940 Munster Final replay a new era opened up for Cork. In March 1941 they won the National League when beating Dublin 4-11 to 2-7 in the final at the Athletic Grounds. That too was a portent of things to come as circumstances would bring the two teams together again at the end of September when Cork would join Tipperary and Kilkenny on the All-Ireland roll of honour with 12 titles each.

Tipperary were drawn to play Waterford in Thurles on the first Sunday in June. However, as foot and mouth disease spread dramatically in May, the game was postponed and re-scheduled for the end of July. Tipperary won the game and expected to play Cork in the Munster semi-final in Limerick in August. A week before the game the Department of Agriculture issued an instruction that the match would not be played.

Although Tipperary, amongst others, asked that the All-Ireland championship be delayed, the Central Council insisted that provinces would nominate teams to play in the All-Ireland series. The Munster Council decided that Cork and Limerick should play to decide who went through. Cork were easy winners by 8-10 to 3-2.

In Leinster, the situation was no easier. Kilkenny were not allowed play in the Leinster final because of the extent of foot and mouth disease in the county so Dublin went through to the All-Ireland semi-final against Galway. The Dublin team still had some representatives of the All-Ireland winning team of 1938, including Laois native Harry Gray whom Lynch described later as one of his favourite players.

1941

IRISH INDEPENDENT

CORK TAKE TWO TITLES AT CROKE PARK

Jim Barry had put the Cork players through a tough training regime to ensure that nothing would be left to chance. By the early stages of the final the difference between the two teams was apparent. As Cork captain Connie Buckley said afterwards, 'I expected a much closer call from Dublin. We were far too speedy for them.'

1941 All-Ireland champions.

Front row: *C. Ring, C. Cottrell.*

Centre row: *W. Campbell, D.J. Buckley, J. Buttimer, J. Quirke, W. Murphy, J. Young.*

Back row: *J. Barry, C. Buckley, M. Brennan, A. Lotty, J. Lynch, B. Thornhill, J. Barrett, T. O'Sullivan, W. Walsh.*

The war-time fuel shortages meant that only 26,150 spectators went to the game. They were treated to a comprehensive display by Cork which overwhelmed Dublin. They were 1-2 to 0-0 ahead after six minutes and by half-time led by 2-8 to 0-3. A 20-year-old Christy Ring had scored three of Cork's points and made a significant impact, described by 'The Recorder' in the Irish Independent the following day as 'one of the stars of the game.' It was one-way traffic for most of the game and Cork were comfortable victors 5-11 to 0-6 at the end.

A feature of the day and cause for celebration in Cork was the fact that the minor team beat Galway in the curtain-raiser by 3-11 to 1-1.

Jack Lynch's first All-Ireland medal was an ambition realised. He had been Cork's captain in 1938-39 and '40 and he hoped that one day he would captain Cork to All-Ireland glory. The opportunity arose in 1942 when he again assumed the role. Other changes were made to the Cork team as the championship got underway. Three young men, Seán Condon, Con Murphy and Mick Kennefick, were brought onto the team. Ned Porter took over in goal from Jim Buttimer, and Paddy O'Donovan became Lynch's partner in midfield. They would play a very influential role in Cork's march to another title.

Although Cork had lost to Tipperary in the delayed Munster final of 1941, the players felt that the real danger to their prospects of winning another All-Ireland championship was Limerick. If they got over that hurdle they felt they would dispose of the Tipperary challenge and march on towards another All-Ireland. In the Munster championship, Limerick were defeated by just two points, a game Jim Young described as 'the best I have ever played in'. In the final, Tipperary were brushed aside as the O'Donovan/Lynch partnership got into full swing. Cork won by 4-15 - 4-1. They then enjoyed an easy win over Galway to qualify for the final.

After the events of the previous year it might have been expected that Dublin would spend a time in transition. In fact, they trounced Kilkenny in the Leinster final by 4-8 to 1-4 and arrived back in Croke Park on All-Ireland final day determined to show everyone that the performance of the previous year was not a true reflection of their worth.

Dublin had a new goalkeeper. Jim Donegan, who later played against Cork in the 1946 and '47 finals for Kilkenny, took over and had an outstanding final. Frank White was the captain and was one of Dublin's best players on the day.

1941, Dublin team.

Front row: *F. White, C. McMahon, E. O'Boyle, C. Downes, P. Farrell, E. Wade, M. Gill, H. Gray.*

Back row: *D. Conway, C. Forde, J. Byrne, T. Leahy, P. McSweeney, G. Glenn,*

D. Nicholl, M. Connolly, M. McDonnell, J. Roche, E. O'Brien, D. Devitt, R. O'Brien.

1942

THE CORK EXAMINER

CORK'S 13th TITLE

Record As Gallant Dublin Bid Fails

Cork 2–14   Dublin 3–4

This was a vastly different game from the previous year, with Dublin battling mightily before succumbing. It was Cork's thirteenth All-Ireland title and took them to the top of the honours list. 'Green Flag' in the *Irish Press* wrote: 'This honour of overstepping Tipperary and Kilkenny was, however, not won without a magnificent struggle in which Dublin played with grand dash and fire, it being only in the closing stages that the Leemen asserted that measure of superiority which kept the title in the south for another year'.

Cork led at half time by 1–7 to 2–1. Jim Donegan showed great skill in the Dublin goal. Twice denying Seán Condon goals with superb saves. Lynch was the master at midfield leading 'Green Flag' to report: 'All through this half the challengers were outclassed at centre-field where Jack Lynch ruled the roost, and it was a splendid performance to hold the champions to so close a margin with this handicap.'

Blarney, 1942. On the way home with the McCarthy Cup.

In the *Irish Independent* the correspondent, 'The Recorder' wrote: 'All round Cork excelled in speed and ball control. Without striking their best form Lynch and O'Donovan had the better of the exchanges with the Dublin pair, Wade and Gray, at midfield and supremacy in this department alone was a telling factor for Cork who had a clever half forward line in Ring, Condon and Kennefick.'

White was moved to midfield for Dublin for the second half with Ned Wade going to the half forward line. It made a difference for Dublin as they narrowed the margin to just two points. But Wade missed a good goal chance and Cork seemed to come alive. John Quirke began to make a telling impact and it was he who began the move that led to the decisive goal, kicked to the net by Derry Beckett. It allowed Cork cruise in the final minutes and they were 2-14 to 3-4 ahead at the end.

Thoughts almost immediately turned to the possibility of a third title in succession. It was a feat achieved only once before by the county (1892-93 and '94) and would act as a great spur to a team that would be led by Mick Kennefick.

Cork's great rivals, Limerick, were beaten by Waterford in the Munster championship and Cork duly qualified for the All-Ireland final but could never have expected that their opponents would come from Ulster. As they were not regarded as a major hurling force.

Again, wartime in Europe had played a part in the destiny of Ireland's young hurlers. The All-Ireland junior championship was suspended. Antrim were the Ulster junior champions and were given the opportunity to play Galway in the All-Ireland quarter final. Antrim caused a mild surprise by winning that game with the odd scoreline of 7-0 to 6-2, with Danny McAllister scoring four goals, but caused an absolute sensation when they beat Kilkenny in the All-Ireland semi-final. The game was played in Corrigan Park and Kilkenny returned home to a hostile reception.

Cork, 1942 All-Ireland Hurling Champions.

Front row: *C. Tobin, C. Murphy, D.J. Buckley, J. Lynch (Capt.), S. Condon, M. Kennefick, J. Quirke, D. Beckett, C. Ring.*

Back Row: *B. Thornhill, P. O'Donovan, W. Murphy, A. Lotty, E. Porter, J. Young, J. Barry (Trainer).*

1943

IRISH INDEPENDENT

CORK'S MASTERLY HURLING

Cork 5–6   **Antrim 0–4**

The final, however, saw a dose of reality injected into Antrim's hearts and minds. 'Antrim came to Croke Park, saw and learned a lesson in hurling from the masters of the game' reported the *Irish Independent* on the morning after the game under the scoreline Cork 5-16, Antrim 0-4. It had been windy in Dublin and Antrim were forced to play against that wind in the first half making a difficult job ever harder. The wind then eased to Cork's advantage in the second half, by which time the contest was already over, Cork having led at half-time by 3-11 to 0-2. Seán Condon had opened the scoring from the throw-in and the avalanche was unstoppable.

Kevin Armstrong later recalled the bitter disappointment felt by the Antrim players.

> We were played off the field by one of the greatest hurling teams ever, but the big disappointment was that we did not do ourselves justice. We were far too inexperienced and completely overcome by the occasion and the place. (The attendance at the game was 48,843, only 2,392 short of the 1936 record).
>
> Croke Park was awesome to us. The surface was perfect and allowed the Cork players display all their artistry. We had come from playing on the bumpy surface of Corrigan Park. We realised immediately that for our standards to improve we would have to become accustomed to playing on better surfaces. It was agreed after the final to develop a new ground in the county and that led to the opening of Casement Park a decade later.

1943 All-Ireland final, Cork vs Antrim.

Dr Mageean, Bishop of Down and Connor, throws in the ball, watched by
Seamus Gardiner, President of the GAA and referee Dr J.J. Stuart. Jack Lynch is
ready for action.

By now the Cork team was attaining a lofty status in the game. They were
favourites to win again in 1944 and become the first team ever to win four
All-Ireland senior hurling titles in a row. Seán Condon, just 21, captained
the team in their bid for history and there were a few changes. Con Cottrell
joined Jack Lynch in midfield and Joe Kelly, a minor medal winner in 1941,
returned to action for his county. Kelly was a clerical student whose
sporting activities were severely curtailed by his vocation. Yet he would
become a great hero for Cork supporters by the end of 1944, a year in
which he also became an Irish sprint champion.

The 1943 Antrim team.

Front row: *J. Maguire, T. Walsh, S. Quinn, S. Mulholland, J. Walsh (Capt.) K. Armstrong, P. McKeown, N. Campbell, W. Best, P. McGarry.*

Back row: *T. Crummey, T. Best, J. McNeill, J. Currie, K. Murphy, D. McAllister, T. McAllister, J. Bateson, J. Hurl, B. McAteer, D. Boylan, J. Butler, J. Mullan, D. McKillop, S. Stinson.*

1944

IRISH INDEPENDENT

CORK HURLERS RETAIN THEIR ALL-IRELAND TITLE

As usual Cork faced their biggest test in Munster. Once again, Limerick provided the toughest opposition and in one of the most memorable Munster finals ever played, it took a spectacular solo goal by Christy Ring in the final minute to separate the two teams in a replay.

Lynch and John Quirke were forced to miss the All-Ireland semi-final because of injury and Cork felt at a loss. Galway were not expected to put up such a challenge but Cork had to battle all the way, Seán Condon scored a total of eight points as they scraped through by 1-10 to 3-3. Dublin were the opposition in the final, having comfortably beaten Antrim in the semi-final.

1944, All-Ireland final, Cork vs Dublin.

Jack Lynch and 'Mucky' Maher tussle for possession at the throw-in, carefully watched by Ned Wade, Frank White, Seán Condon, Jim Young and Mick Ryan. Referee: Mick Hennessy (Clare).

Again, wartime restrictions meant that the attendance at the final on September 3 was just below 27,000. The Dublin team was sprinkled with familiar and highly-respected players such as Ned Wade, Charlie Downes, Frank White, Harry Gray and goalkeeper Jim Donegan. For ten minutes Dublin held Cork scoreless. Lynch then opened the scoring and a pattern began to emerge. By half-time Cork led by 0-8 to 0-2.

The *Irish Press* newspaper reported:

> At centre-field Lynch and Con Cottrell struck up a marvellously successful partnership and their sound and spectacular feats paved the way for the forwards to get the all-important scores. The Cork defence was very sound and could in no way be blamed for the goal scored by Dublin. The Cork forwards individually and collectively were magnificent in every movement and proved they were equal, if not superior, to any set of forwards sent out by the Rebel County.

1944 All-Ireland Champions.

Front row: *J. Young, J. Lynch, S. Condon (Capt.), J. Morrison, C. Cottrell, C. Ring, D.J. Buckley.*

Back row: *W. Walsh, J. Quirke, C. Murphy, A. Lotty, W. Murphy, J. Kelly, T. Mulcahy, P. O'Donovan, B. Thornhill, J. Barry.*

Kelly delighted the Cork supporters with his thrilling solo runs, while Mulcahy also won the plaudits of the supporters. Both players were chaired off the field after Cork, had won convincingly again by 2-13 to 1-2. The team was treated to a heroes welcome on its return to Cork. Nine players had played in all four All-Ireland victories; Lynch, Willie Murphy, Batt Thornhill, Alan Lotty, John Quirke, Christy Ring, D.J. Buckley and Jim Young. Paddy O'Donovan had played in 1942 and 1944 and came on as a sub in 1941 and 1943.

While Jack Lynch would win an All-Ireland football medal in 1945, the hurlers unbeaten run came to an end when they lost to Tipperary in the Munster championship. Any thoughts that the team was finished were dispelled in 1946. Jim Barry had not given up hope of another championship success and Cork prepared diligently for the Munster campaign. They beat

Clare, Waterford and a disappointing Limerick team to qualify for an All-Ireland semi-final clash with Galway. This was another comfortable success and on September 1 Cork renewed rivalry with Kilkenny in the All-Ireland final for the first time since the famous final in 1939.

CORK'S FOUR IN A ROW
(Cors. O'Connell)

1.
You'll find in Gaelic history
Hurlers of great fame,
Of deeds they've done, of honours won
And how they played the game.
The boys that brought us history
To live for evermore,
Were the boys that came from rebel Cork
In nineteen forty-four.

Chorus
Some came from St Finbarrs,
From 'Sars' Blackrock and Glen,
From Valley Rovers, Buttevant,
To help in Cork's fourth win,
From Ballincollig, UCC
The all joined in the work,
The boys that broke all records were
The boys of the County Cork.

2.
In Cork's drawn game with Limerick
It looked a Limerick win,
With the Corkmen's backs against the wall,
They fought Mick Mackey's men,
When victory seemed beyond their reach
No man was known to shirk
When the crowd roars, they're even scores,
That great goal by John Quirke.
Chorus

3.
We'll ne'er forget that Thurles game
That memorable day
When Cork and Limerick clashed once more
In that grand Munster replay;
And when the teams had equalised,
The crowd did shout and sing,
At that solo run, and winning goal
By the 'Glen' man Christy Ring.
Chorus

4.
When at Ennis against Galway
They were caught in a pinch,
That day they played without the aid
Of John Quirke and Jack Lynch.
Then their skipper, young Seán Condon,
Rose to great heights that day,
With steady aim he shot the point
That saved Cork in the fray.
Chorus

5.
When at Croke Park, Cork met Dublin
Each man will trained and fit
From the goalie, to full forward,
Each Corkman did his bit.
Andwhen history is written
Of those fearless hurling men,
You'll find the lad that thrilled 'Croke Park',
Joe Kelly of the Glen.
Chorus

1946

The Cork Examiner's headline read: 'Ring's wonder goal kept title in Cork.'

An attendance of 64,415 turned up for the final. The stands had been pre-booked and so great was the demand for sideline seats that the gates at Croke Park were closed an hour before the senior final began, with approximately 5,000 spectators locked out.

1946 All-Ireland Champions.

With an overcast sky and mist falling on the morning of the game, the pitch was very wet and the conditions made it very difficult for the players. *The Cork Examiner* reported: 'The pitch in the early stages favoured the defences, and the slippery state of it led to a number of frees, mostly of a technical nature, such as a player falling, and putting his hand on an opponent's back to save himself.'

Christy Ring had led Cork onto the field to the usual great roar and he would leave supporters gasping in awe just before half-time with one of the greatest goals in the history of All-Ireland finals. Cork were leading by 1-3 to 0-5 when lost time was being played. Paddy O'Donovan had cleared his lines and the ball fell to Ring about 70 yards from the Kilkenny posts. Picking up the ball in his usual smart fashion, he started a solo run with the ball hopping on his hurley and Jack Mulcahy, the Kilkenny captain who was playing a grand game, almost at his heels. For the first ten yards the Kilkenny man seemed to be gaining but then Ring began to draw away. As he drew close to the Kilkenny posts Walsh and Butler made a dash for him but the Cork captain side-stepped them cleverly and got within five yards or so when he deftly placed the ball with a neat flick out of Donegan's reach for one of the grandest of the many great goals he scored in his career.'

For Jim Donegan, who had already lost two All-Ireland finals in the Dublin colours against Cork, this was another frustrating day. By the end he had conceded seven goals: Cork won by 7-5 to 3-8. At one stage during the second half Kilkenny had reduced the deficit to just two points, Terry Leahy scoring two goals, but Cork ran riot at the end.

The achievement had been spectacular – five All-Ireland championships out of six. For Lynch, it was six championships in a row. The hurlers were now being regarded as one of the greatest teams of all time. And the irony was that the best was probably to come before the team broke up but they would not add another All-Ireland title.

1947

IRISH INDEPENDENT

KILKENNY WIN THIRTEENTH TITLE

Kilkenny 0–14   **Cork 2–7**

The 1947 All-Ireland final is generally regarded as one of the greatest ever played. Cork had been regarded as lucky to beat Limerick by three points in the Munster final and had enjoyed an easy victory over Antrim in the All-Ireland semi-final.

Kilkenny All-Ireland Senior Hurling Champions 1947.

Back row: *T. Walsh (Chairman Co. Board), N. O'Donnell, T. Murphy, S. Downey, J. Mulcahy, J. Langton, N. Kavanagh, T. Leahy, T. Walton, J. Heffernan, J. Kelly, B. Walsh.*

Centre row: *M. Dalton (trainer), L. Reidy, M. Marnell, P. Hayden, D. Kennedy (Capt.), P. Prendergast, B. Cahill, P. Grace, S. Bluett.*

Front row: *M. Joyce, J. Egan, J. Donegan, P. Lennon, P. O'Brien.*

Just over 61,000 spectators packed into Croke Park on a pleasant day. They were unaware of the drama unfolding below them in the dressing-room when Bill Walsh was forced to cry off the Kilkenny team and Jim Heffernan was called in. Kilkenny's captain, Paddy Grace chose not to take part in the pre-match parade as he had a knee injury.

Kilkenny had decided on their tactics in advance. Their knowledge of the quality of the Cork defence – Alan Lotty, Paddy O'Donovan, Willie Murphy, Jim Young, DJ Buckley and Con Murphy as well as goalkeeper Tom Mulcahy – meant that they would not go for goals but would settle for points. It ensured a most unimaginable nail-biting and dramatic finale to the game.

Kilkenny led by 0-7 to 0-5 after a titanic first-half struggle. Cork moved Jack Lynch to wing forward and brought Seán Condon to midfield. In a pulsating half hour Cork scored two goals, the second by Joe Kelly giving them a one point lead as the game entered its dying moments.

Kilkenny were awarded a free about 30 yards from the Cork goal. Terry Leahy moved the ball from where the referee had placed it and the Cork players felt a free out should be awarded. The referee, Phil Purcell of Tipperary, replaced the ball again and allowed Leahy take the free. Although Kilkenny were behind, he opted for the safety of the equalising score. 'It was very tempting to go for goal' he later recalled, 'but I had to resist it'.

His patience would be rewarded. A long puck out was gathered by Paddy Grace who drove the ball towards the Cork goal. Leahy takes up the story:

> Jim Langton hit the ball into the Cork goalie and he cleared it out to the Hill 16 side. I ran ahead of Alan Lotty and got the ball and put it between the posts. Jack Lynch had an opportunity for an equaliser but was hooked twice by desperate defenders. Kilkenny held out for a 0-14 to 2-7 victory in a hurling classic.

It brought to an end one of the most glorious eras in hurling history.

10

The Football Years

Tim Horgan

ON A BITTERLY cold and wet November day in 1938, St Nicks and Clonakilty were dourly contesting the county final on a mucky pitch known as the 'Bog in Bandon'. Conditions were so bad that by half-time only one score had been recorded, a Bobby Buckle goal for St Nicks. Earlier in the game the Clon football had gone out of action but the match continued with the St Nicks' ball. The Blackpool men were doing well and victory was in sight after a second Bobby Buckle goal placed them 2-1 to 0-2 ahead. Then, to their utter dismay, the wind carried a powerful Clon clearance by Mick Finn into the nearby stream which was in full spate. As a section of the large crowd gazed aghast at the ball being swept away, it was inevitable that the match would be abandoned. One man, however, had different ideas – the St Nicks' centre-back ~~~~ mates were close to an historic county double and there was ~~~~ going to be denied it. Into the water Jack plunged and swam powerfully to retrieve the football. As spectators watched in amazement he reached the ball and brought it back. The game resumed and Jack Lynch, dripping wet, continued his role in defence. St Nicks went on to win the match and capture their first senior county title and complete the double for Blackpool for the first time.

Fittingly, it was the brave young man from the Shandon district who was given the honour of captaining the Cork footballers the following year. He was also Cork's hurling captain in 1939 and thus became possibly the only man in history to captain both Cork teams in the one year. Jack's football career reflected a period of unprecedented success for both his club and his county. Although St Nicks had been very active in the early years of the century, the club fell on hard times in the 1920s before a revival occurred in the early 1930s. Jack, still a teenager, was on the team that reached the intermediate final of 1934 only to lose to Bantry. Three years later, St Nicks won the intermediate championship, beating Bantry after a replay, and they went senior in 1938. He won the first of his two senior football medals that year, his second in 1941. 'It's a funny thing,' said Jack, 'but I always felt at a loss on the football field. I didn't know what to do with my hands, being so used to holding a hurley. It was a strange feeling which one got over only after many, many matches'. Dave Creedon recalls:

> Jack was a very good footballer. He was two years older than me but we played minor together in 1934 and were team-mates for the Glen and St Nicks for almost 20 years. I started in goal for the seniors, but I later moved to midfield and got to know his play very well. He was tall and strong, but never dirty. I remember one match late in his career when his opponents did anything and everything to him but Jack refused to be provoked.

Jim Murphy, a Tralee-born gárda who captained the winning Kerry team in 1953, recalls:

> Playing football for Nicks was an unusual experience in those days. They didn't have the catch and kick style so common then, but they were very devilish. Most of them were hurlers and, when we'd go up to the Glen field for training, it would be all hurling. A few others and myself would have to find a football and a little spot at the corner of the field to do our bit of training. If there was a big match coming up, we'd have two or three nights' football training and we'd get treated to milk and buns afterwards in the old Glen clubroom at Bird's Quay. Jack Lynch was one of the best hurlers I've ever seen, and he was also a very good footballer. He was very strong and was able to use himself in the right way. When 'shouldering' an opponent, he was a topper, but he was always fair. He had a lovely temperament on and off the field.

1937 Intermediate Champions.

Front row: *J. Daly, B. Buckle, J. Buckley, D. Creedon, P. Burke, P. Callaghan, T. Kiely.*

Back row: *D.M. Dorgan, C. Buckley, J. Lynch, J. O'Sullivan, B. Culhane, D. Moylan, C. Tobin, P. O'Donovan.*

1938

St Nicks' victory in the 1938 county final marked a watershed in his career. He would play in four county football finals altogether and help Cork to win two Munster championships and a long-awaited All-Ireland title. The 1941 county final pitted St Nicks against Millstreet at Macroom.

THE CORK EXAMINER

It was an intensive struggle, very robust with hard knocks given and taken in a sporting spirit. Two points by Jack Lynch and one each by Bobby Buckle, Charlie Tobin and Dan 'Cooper' Moylan had St Nicks in front 0-5 to 0-4 at half-time, the Millstreet points coming from O'Connor and Kiely. Millstreet went ahead with an O'Leary goal in the second half but Joe Looney retaliated for St Nicks who led by two points as the game drew to a close. Then Jack Lynch scored his third point and St Nicks won their second county title, 1-8 to 1-5.

Fourteen of the players had already won senior hurling championship medals with the Glen to complete the double once more.

Golden Jubilee Celebration of 1938 County Championship victory.

Front row: B. Buckle, P. Collins, D.J. Buckley, C. Tobin, D. Moylan, D. Creedon.

Back row: T. Kiely, P. Hogan, J. Lynch, B. Culhane, C. Buckley, P. Burke, P. O'Donovan, P. Barry.

1947

Jim Cronin and Jack Lynch lead out the teams, St Nicks vs Army, 1947 County football semi-final. Over 10,000 spectators attended at the Camp field.

1947 County football final, St Nicks vs Clonakilty.

Front row: *S. Linehan, J. Looney, J. Hartnett, J. Lynch (Capt.), P. Hogan, J. Lyons, D. Twomey, D. Creedon, D. O'Donovan, P. O'Regan.*

Back row: *M. McInerney, P. O'Donovan, J. Farnan, J. Murphy, E. Byrnes, D. Owens, J. Lynam, J. Cremen, J. Murphy, J. Kelly, W. O'Sullivan, T. Normoyle, S. Daly, D.J. Buckley, M. O'Brien.*

County Football

Breakthrough in '43

For many years football was very much the poor relation of hurling in Cork. While the county hurlers were delighting supporters with consecutive All-Ireland victories, the footballers languished in the background, eliciting little interest among the general public. Then came a major breakthrough in 1943, as surprising as it was welcome.

THE CORK EXAMINER

A strange thing happened on Sunday. A very large gathering of Cork Gaels actually got intensely excited during the Cork and Kerry football match in the Munster championship. Ever since 1911, the standard of the game has deteriorated in Cork to such an extent that there was never any real excitement when a Cork football team was engaged. Those at the Park last Sunday saw a Cork team that was certainly a revelation.

1943 Cork team.

Front row: *L. Aherne, E. Casey, J. Lynch.*

Centre row: *J. Kenny, S. Minogue, N. Duggan, T. Crowley, J. Aherne, E. Young, G. O'Leary, J. Young, J. Barry, M. Murphy.*

Back row: *W. Walsh, M. O'Mahoney, P. O'Donovan, D. Magnier, R. Harnedy, P. Cronin, D. O'Connor, J. Cronin, A. Scannell, E. Courtney, P. O'Grady, P. A. Murphy, F. O'Donovan, D. J. Murphy, S. McCarthy, T. O'Reilly.*

Jack Lynch, one of the few city players on the team, had a big part to play in Cork's resurgence that year. Cork drew with Kerry in the semi-final and caused even greater surprise when they won the replay by a point, 1-5 to 1-4. 'Eamonn Young and Jack Lynch were flashing in at opportune moments,' wrote *The Cork Examiner*, 'and the Kerry backs were bombarded. It was the same pair that initiated Cork's winning point. Young and Lynch led one final assault and Casey swung a perfect ball well above the bar to finish a great display.' This was Cork's first defeat of Kerry in over 30 years and it was greeted with great excitement.

Fermoy was the venue for the Munster final, and after a hard game Cork beat Tipperary 1-7 to 1-4 and Jack added a football medal to the hurling medals he had already won.

So it was on to Croke Park to meet the mighty Cavan team, football kingpins of their time. Cork played with the wind from the start but showed their inexperience by wasting numerous chances. 'From good ground,' wrote *The Cork Examiner*, 'score after score was lost until Jack Lynch, from a grand catch and swing, turned in a point high in the battlements'. That score settled the Cork side, Jim Cronin added a great goal and Jack Lynch got another point to place them 1-5 to 0-3 ahead at the break.'

A goal by Stafford brought Cavan to the fore in the second half but Cork battled gamely to the end. 'Cork's last challenge against the wind brought the biggest thrill of the hour,' wrote *The Cork Examiner*. 'Lynch, Young, Casey, Duggan and Minogue were upfield, Benson and Cully were tested. Cavan's goal all but fell twice in succession. 30,000 men were on tiptoe watching the canal goal. Aherne narrowed the gap from a short angle. One point behind. In a great effort to turn in a crossing ball, Aherne crashed into the posts. Cavan's fine backs rallied round, the ball was cleared to midfield and referee Brendan Nestor blew full-time.'

So Cork's unexpected resurgence in 1943 ended in a one-point defeat, 1-8 to 1-7 in the All-Ireland semi-final. Although Jack would win his third hurling medal a few weeks later, he shared the bitter disappointment of his colleagues who sensed that this was a game they should have won. The following year the footballers lost their Munster title to Tipperary, and many supporters despaired of ever seeing the Sam Maguire cup in the rebel county. But the Cork football scene was about to change dramatically with the heroic deeds of the '45 team led by 'Tadhgo' Crowley.

THE CORK EXAMINER

CORK'S THRILLING VICTORY, 1945 MUNSTER FINAL

Day of Shock Results

Cork 1–11   **Kerry 1–6**

Cork got off to a blistering start at Killarney with a point by Derry Beckett and a goal from Eamonn Young inside the first five minutes. They led by three points at half-time and, with the midfielders on top and the forwards dominant, Cork led by five points entering the last quarter.

Then Kerry redoubled their efforts, and they literally ran themselves to a standstill in trying to reduce the gap. Time and again the huge crowds were brought to their toes by passages of beautiful football from both sides. A great Kerry rally was rewarded when Lyne had another point and, at this stage, Tubridy thrilled the crowd with a grand solo run which was finished by Jack Lynch snapping the ball into the net, but the goal was disallowed. Despite that, Cork went on to score a famous victory over the Kingdom, 1-11 to 1-6.

Cork faced Galway in the All-Ireland semi-final without the great full back 'Weeshie' Murphy, whose brother Fr Con had died after a short illness in West Africa. 'Cork missed "Weesh" at Croke Park,' wrote 'Carbery', 'yet this great-hearted side rose to the occasion and played their best game in decades. Croke Park's sward was like polished velvet. Galway's jerseys were changed to white – Cork's red and white was the longer registered – and the great game opened before 35,000 eager spectators. They got full value for their money. Galway were away and McManus opened. Jack Lynch, brainy as ever, made a delightful opening for Derry Beckett who flashed to the net. Sergeant Cronin's swinging point put Cork a goal clear and after many fine bouts of true orthodox Gaelic football, Fachtna O'Donovan of

Ross used his towering height to punch home Cork's second goal at the end of the first quarter.'

Cork continued to play fast, lively football but a Johnny Canavan goal reduced the lead to two points, 2-2 to 1-3 at half-time. On the resumption, Cork again took the initiative, as 'Carbery' so vividly described in the *Cork Weekly Examiner*:

CORK WEEKLY EXAMINER

That pocket Hercules from Dunmanway, Eamonn Young, opened up his elusive play, handled and swerved, paving the way for two grand points off his boot before sending the flashing Clare boy, Tubridy, home for another. Then came an astonishing Galway rally. They swept down like an Atlantic gale from Aran. Charlie Connolly dummied through and goaled. Thousands of westerners opened a storm of cheering as McManus and O'Sullivan, with three glorious points, set the teams level for the first time. With the Galway supporters roaring their team home the Cork selectors, aided by some Kerry friends, got to work on the switches. They brought Jack Lynch, a fresh brainy man, from outfield. He soon made his presence felt. Beckett notched a minor, McManus again balanced, but Cork now took a determined hold of the game. The captain, Tadhgo Crowley of Clon, had been their pillar throughout. He never erred. He drove long, confident balls to his front lines and he broke up every dangerous raid. Casey now shone, Tubridy flashed through for a Cork goal (disallowed) but Derry Beckett pointed and Cronin, with two beautifully delivered balls dead over the crossbar, put Cork well clear. Beckett, now deadly accurate, had another brace and when Ryan had Galway's final point, the great game was over. Five hundred joint followers treated the 30 players to a big supper and reception at Clery's ballroom where wit and wine of the nation's genius ran high.

THE CORK EXAMINER

CORK REGAIN THE FOOTBALL TITLE AFTER THIRTY-FOUR YEARS

Great Defence Weathers Thrilling Cavan Rally

Cork 2–5   **Cavan 0–7**

The All-Ireland final aroused enormous interest throughout the city and county. Not only had more than three decades elapsed since Cork's last appearance in a final but for the first time in five years the Cork hurlers had failed to come out of Munster. The footballers were the county's sole standard-bearers.

Jack Lynch arrived late at Croke Park due to traffic problems, but pre-match panic was to prove a blessing in disguise. He was so concerned at getting to the game that he forgot about the big match jitters most players endure. 'I was just relieved to be on the pitch on time and I was calm, composed and, above all, relieved when the match started.' Not surprisingly, he went on to play a great game.

'From the moment the ball was thrown in until the final whistle, there was not a moment of play which was without its thrills,' wrote *The Cork Examiner*. 'The Cork fifteen, giving a display of hard, keen football which kept their huge hosting of supporters in a frenzy of excitement, achieved a great and well deserved victory'.

1945 Cork team.

Top: *T. Crowley (Capt.)*

Left (reading down): *D. Magnier, F. O'Donovan, J. Lynch, P. Cronin.*

Right (reading down): *M. Tubridy, M. O'Driscoll, D. O'Connor, E. Young.*

Bottom: *P. Murphy, J. Cronin, D. Beckett, E. Casey, C. Crone, H. O'Neill.*

Cork were just a point in front of Cavan when the decisive piece of action occurred near the end, as Eamonn Andrews, the well-known broadcaster, reported:

> Jack Lynch got the ball, booted it to Jim Cronin who nonplussed the Cavan backs by hand-passing it back to the ever-alert Derry Beckett. Beckett wasted no time and sent the ball rattling against the net. From that time on, Cork held on to their opponents with a grip of steel. Cavan struggled and fought, but they had met their masters. It may have been my imagination, but I thought the Cusack Stand trembled when the final whistle went, and thousands of Cork fans roared and whistled, sang and cheered.

The Sam Maguire returns to Cork.
Tadhgo Crowley, captain, holds the All-Ireland cup aloft.

The scenes that followed the final whistle were ones of immense joy for Cork as the captain, 'Tadhgo' Crowley, was mobbed and lifted shoulder high by delirious supporters. Sunday September 23, 1945 was a day of supreme glory for the Cork footballers who won the Sam Maguire Cup. A dream had come true for the players, their mentors and supporters, but who could have imagined such a happy end when Cork began the championship four months earlier.

1945 Cavan Team.

Front row: *B. O'Reilly, P. Smith, J. Boylan, P.J Duke, T. O'Reilly (Capt.), S. Deignan, T.P. O'Reilly, J. J. O'Reilly, P. Reilly, J. Stafford.*

Back row: *H. Smyth, D. O'Reilly, D. R. McGovern, P. Doyle, P. Brady, J. Wilson, P. P. Galligan, P. Donohoe, T. Tighe, B. Kelly, M. Higgins, B. Cully, H. O'Reilly, J. W. Martin, F. Comiskey.*

Sam Maguire Comes Home

'Carbery', in his *Cork Weekly Examiner*, wrote:

> Thirty-four years – half a lifetime – since Cork won a football All-Ireland! That explains why I laughed and defied the fierce 'nor wester' shower that swept Croke Park as the immense

good-humoured throng were smoothing away after as exciting an hour's football as you could wish to see. A West-Cork relative, who had travelled 230 miles, stuck a red and white goose quill in my hat as I mounted my trusty bike. Sane people were wondering who was the wild 'mountaineer' with the raking red goose quill out of his hat and rising a 'strouncawn' of Land League days:

> *One evening of late as I happened to stray*
> *Bound for Clonakilty from sweet Timoleague,*
> *'Twas at Ballinscarthy some time I delayed,*
> *I wetted my whistle with porter.*
> *I kindled my pipe and I spat on my stick,*
> *I kept the Coach Road, like a deer I did trip,*
> *I cared for no bailiff, landlord or Old Nick,*
> *I sang like a lark in the morning.*

Carbery's delight at the Clon-inspired Cork victory was shared by his neighbours back home. 'Clonakilty won the county in 1942, '43, '44 and again in '46 and '47,' said Tom Lyons. 'In the year they missed out they won the All-Ireland instead. Well, that's what Clonakilty people have always claimed and, even if it is stretching the truth a little, who can really contradict it? With nine players on the panel – six of them playing in the final – and four selectors, Clon can surely lay claim to being the inspiration behind that great triumph.'

WHEN CLON CAME HOME
By 'Carbery'

1

One evening of late bonfires blazed in the sky,
And the townsmen and neighbours in
thousands stood by,
Young maidens sang, waving their
banners on high
Three cheers for the Clon. boys and Erin.
Our brass bands and pipers played
gallant and gay,
My heart leapt with joy that I came by this way,
For the Cork lads had landed at home on that day
With the cup that our Tadhgo was wavin'.

Chorus

Long life to our champions from
Glanworth to Clare
From Beara to Youghal and home thro' Banteer,
At Kilmichael, with Barry, we never knew fear
Agus fágaimid siúd mar atá sé

2

'Twas up at Croke Park on last
Sunday, we hear,
That Corkmen faced Cavan, whose
fame was so dear,
Those northmen were good and our
scores they ran near,
But we held them, and led them and beat them.
'Twas Beckett's grand goal, sure, that
finished the fray,
And Tubridy's pace was the talk of the day,
But our backs were like granite, where Weeshie
held sway
With Crowley and Driscoll to greet them.

Chorus

3

Brave Crone and Dave Magnier from
sweet old Fermoy,
Din Connor, Pat Cronin – our pride
and our joy.
Ross Fachtna O'Donovan, rangy and coy,
And where would you leave
Eamonn Young boys!
He dummied and drove like his father of old,
And showed them some tricks from
Dunmanway, I'm told.
Humphrey Neill and Jack Lynch and
Jim Cronin so bold
Set our heroes like deerhounds in tongue boys.

Chorus

4

'Togher' Casey was marking his man
near the hour,
Hand-and-foot he kept dodging, then
driving with power,
Macroom and Millstreet, and Cork town
– but the flower
Were Weesh and Tadhgo Crowley,
our captain.
So here's to our footballers, fearless and free
Clonakilty, Rosscarbery and famed
Dun-man-wee,
The Sam Maguire Cup has come home
to the Lee
Agus fágaimid siúd mar atá sé.

Cork footballers off to London for the 1946 Whitsun tournament.

Jim Cronin, in an interview with Tom Morrison, recalls:

> Jack collected his sixth consecutive All-Ireland medal in 1946, a unique achievement, but he was part of another bit of history also in 1946. It was the Whit weekend and we were going to London to play Cavan in the Owen Ward football tournament. We set out for Dublin that Sunday morning, stopped at Limerick to watch Cork and Clare in the Munster Championship and collect Jack Lynch, Jim Barry and one or two others. Then we went on to Collinstown aerodrome and we flew out on a DC3. We were the first GAA team ever to travel by plane. We landed at Croydon, played Cavan the next day and lost by a goal. Fr Cremin presented the trophy to the great John Joe O'Reilly. After the match we flew back to Dublin and went home to Cork by car. That historic flight made Jack Lynch the first man to play for Cork in two different countries on the same weekend.

The Manhattan Skyline

An extra dimension was added to the football championship in 1947 when the GAA announced that the All-Ireland final would take place in New York. There was a festive atmosphere at the Park the day of the Munster final with Danny Hobbs leading a singsong in the covered stand, and the St Finbarrs' Pipe Band from Killeens providing rousing tunes.

'It was a sunny day,' recalls Jas Murphy, 'but the pitch was very soggy after the heavy rain that had fallen during the week.' Dr Manning, the Auxiliary Bishop of Los Angeles, threw in the ball to start what was to become one of the most talked-about matches ever played between Cork and Kerry.

Kerry started well and were two goals ahead approaching half-time.

THE CORK EXAMINER

Then the Cork forwards rallied in grand style and following two frees, McGrath sent a lovely centre to the Kerry goal-mouth and the front line forwards swarmed in and in a terrific onslaught Jack Lynch boxed the ball into the net for a well-earned goal. Kerry led 2-5 to 1-5 at the break but, backed by the wind, Cork quickly put on the pressure in the second half. Jim Aherne sent a blistering shot to the net from a 21-yards free and, though still in front near the finish, Kerry had to defend resolutely.

A grand rally by the Cork forwards ended in a free on the 14-yards line. Again, the Cork forwards, according to a pre-arranged plan, tried to rush a goal through but this time the Kerry defence was so severely tested that a penalty kick was awarded against them.

A Cork goal seemed a certainty until it was offset by a magnificent piece of Kerry cuteness, as Eamonn Young recalled:

The Park was very soft and muddy that day and Kerry were on top for most of the game. We made a rally towards the end and were just two points behind when we won a penalty. The referee, Simon Deignan of Cavan, placed the ball for Jim Aherne to take the shot but there was a delay as Jackie Lyne, who had been injured, was carried off around behind the goal. During the hold-up, Joe Keohane moved over to chat with Jim Aherne and, as he did so, he placed his foot on the ball and pressed it firmly into the mud. Now Jim Aherne had a marvellous kick – he had already scored a goal from a 21-yards free – and we all knew he'd score from the penalty. To our astonishment, when he took the penalty, the ball just trickled towards the welcoming hands of Danno Keefe who booted it with glee about 70 yards down the field. In fairness to Joe Keohane, he expressed some remorse to me years later. 'Eamonn,' he said, 'I know it was wrong to push that football deep into the mud that day, but all of a sudden I got a vision of the Manhattan skyline and that's what made me do it'. Kerry won by 3-8 to 2-6 and Joe and his team-mates went on to play Cavan in New York later in the year.

Final Farewell

1951 County final team.

Front row: *S. O'Brien, D. O'Donovan, D. Creedon, P. Martin, J. Lynam, J. Hartnett, C. O'Flaherty, D. Twomey, S. O'Sullivan, D. O'Brien.*

Back row: *S. O'Brien, D. O'Sullivan, M. O'Brien, C. Hewitt, J. Nash, J. Lyons, J. Farnan, G. Linehan, L. Ó Tuama, J. Lynch, S. O'Callaghan, P. Hogan, V. Twomey, P. Hartnett, A. Ó Tuama.*

At the start of his football career, Kerry treated Cork with understandable disdain, but by the time Jack retired with Munster and All-Ireland medals to his credit, the situation was much different. In 1952, Kerry could manage just 2 points against Cork's 11 in the Munster final.

Jack retired following the victory of Glen Rovers in the 1950 county final but a year later, St Nicks reached the county football final against Collins. A key player was suspended after the semi-final against the Guards and the Glen's involvement in the 1951 championship also took its toll with injuries to a number of players. Jack went to the county final as a spectator but the St Nicks' selectors asked him to line out. 'I don't even have gear,' Jack protested, but Mick McCarthy (Langton) quickly acquired shorts, socks and boots for the 34-year-old politician. He gamely took his place at full forward in a match that *The Cork Examiner* described as 'a hard and dour struggle with plenty of hard knocks being given and taken'. Although badly out of condition after his long lay-off from playing, Jack scored a point, set up John Lyons for another and was fouled going through for an easy free which the kicker missed.

He launched my book *Cork's Hurling Story* at the Metropole Hotel early in 1977 and I was talking to him when Christy Ring arrived in the room. They hadn't met for some time and I was curious to see how they'd greet one another. There was no, 'Hello Christy, how are you? How are Rita and the kids?' After perfunctory nods of recognition, Jack went straight to the point. 'What are our chances of winning the county this year?'

During his illustrious playing career he had many memorable homecomings to Blackpool with victorious Cork, Glen and St Nicks teams but perhaps the greatest welcome of all was accorded him in 1966 when he came home as Taoiseach.

Chatting with Christy Ring.

Eamonn Young described the scene:

> Thousands gathered near Dublin Hill to welcome him, and tar barrels blazed outside the clubhouse where two groups of schoolboys, wearing the Glen and St Nicks colours, greeted him by singing Irish ballads. Then, with the crowd surging round him, Jack began to deliver his address.

> 'What's he saying?' asked an old-timer at the back of the crowd. 'Yerra, what's he saying', answered his pal, 'only that he's glad to be home and he'd play for the Glen in the morning if he could'.

11
The Railway Cup

Mick Dunne

A STROLL AROUND the £1 million museum the GAA opened at Croke Park in the new Cusack stand is thoroughly enjoyable and worthwhile, and during which, one is apt to be dazzled by the spectacular array of fascinating items. Among them stands the glittering treasure of gold that is Jack Lynch's impressive and historic accumulation of medals including those he got in the Railway Cup competition. The seven of them form a sparkling line of their own in the glass-case devoted to Jack's collection from an outstanding playing career.

It brings to mind an occasion when I had, however briefly, some of those very same medals actually in my possession. It happened in the early 1980s when a small group of us were asked to organise an exhibition of Gaelic games' memorabilia in conjunction with Féile na nGael which was being held in Dublin. Jack very generously gave us his medals to put on display in a premises made available by the National Museum and it was my good fortune to be the one he charged with getting them there. What a frightening responsibility was placed on me by the second paragraph of the letter sent from his holiday home in Skibbereen: 'I am depending on you for their safe keeping.' Although I recognised the honour of having my hands on them even for a short while, and even though they were exhibited in a security display case, there were some sleepless nights until they were safely deposited back in his possession.

Examining those medals again not long ago in the company of the very helpful administrator of the GAA museum, Donncha Ó Dúlaing junior, one couldn't help but ponder on how Jack Lynch, and indeed his contemporaries, who wore Munster's royal blue with pride when the Railway Cup competitions prospered, must have been dismayed by the sad decline of the interprovincial championships in latter times. Men who represented their provinces before crowds of anything up to 30-40,000 people, even in the Emergency years of seriously restricted travel, must have heard and read with disbelief of matches attended by mere hundreds. It would have been inconceivable to them in the 1940s that the day might ever arrive when a hurling final between Munster and Connacht wouldn't attract more than 487 spectators, in Thurles of all places.

Not so when Jack Lynch first got a Munster jersey. A different time, a different world; so different that only three provinces played in the hurling competition at the time with the result that Munster didn't have a semi-final in 1938 when Jack was first honoured by the province, six months before his 21st birthday. Leinster beat Connacht by 14 points in a replay at Tullamore to qualify for the St Patrick's Day final. When the Munster team was picked for that decider, Jack Lynch's name was listed sixth of the nine substitutes. On the National festival a crowd of 18,120 paid £937 into Croke Park and Leinster led narrowly 2-2 to 2-1 at half-time. At that stage the Munster selectors called upon Jack for the second half and it was reported that he went on to the half-back line with Larry Blake of Clare moving outfield in positional switches. Munster, holders of the Railway Cup, came through a storming second half which was said to have had 'some of the most glorious hurling seen in Croke Park for some time' and they eventually won by five points (6-2 to 4-3), giving Jack Lynch the first of those seven Railway Cup medals.

He added to the collection for the next two years, but each time he was again initially chosen as a sub for the province. In 1939, the team was announced on January 8 with Jack's name last of the five subs, but when John Quirke was injured during the semi-final against Connacht in Birr he was replaced by Jack. However, when Quirke cried off the team to meet

Leinster in the final on March 17, Jim Mullane of Clare was chosen to take his place at right full-forward. Jack wasn't called upon for that final or for the decider of 1940, when Munster beat Leinster both years. In fact, the province had no need for subs in the '39 final which they won by seven points and Waterford's John Keane was the only sub used in the following year's final when he took over from Paddy Clohessy of Limerick.

Ironically, when Jack Lynch was finally chosen to start an interprovincial final it was in the 1941 decider which Munster lost to Leinster, something that had happened only four times in the previous 14 years of the competition. For that year's semi-final against Connacht in Galway, Jack was originally listed fourth on the substitutes' panel, immediately behind one Christy Ring. Peadar Flanagan of Tipperary cried-off before the match and Jack was the replacement at right half-forward. He scored Munster's fifth and sixth goals in an easy victory, 7-5 to 0-6. By now the shortages of fuel caused by World War II rationing were being severely felt around the country and travel was very restricted, so when St Patrick's Day '41 fell on a Monday the Central Council decided to stage the Railway Cup finals on the Sunday, March 16. The Monday programme at Croke Park consisted of the All-Ireland Colleges' interprovincial hurling final and a Dublin club camogie tie, UCD vs Coláiste San Dominic. Incidentally, in that colleges' match two of the outstanding figures in a Connacht victory over Munster were Colm Corless, who would be centre half-back on an all-Galway team in the Railway Cup final eight years later, and Bill Carlos, an All-Ireland football medallist with Roscommon in 1943 and '44.

Jack Lynch's performance in Galway earned him retention at right half-forward when the Munster team was announced for the final but he actually lined-out against Leinster at centre half because of the late withdrawal of the Limerick brothers, John and Mick Mackey. It was a triple-decker programme on March 16 with a colleges' football semi-final, Ulster vs Munster first at 1.15pm, the Ulster–Munster Railway Cup football final at 2.30pm and the hurling decider at 3.45pm. Despite the problems with transport it attracted 20,123 to Croke Park. Munster won the two football games but were deprived of the treble when the hurlers were pipped by

Leinster by one solitary point, 2-5 to 2-4. A late goal and point by the great Jimmy Langton of Kilkenny edged Leinster into a lead that Munster couldn't erase despite a Jackie Power goal and John Quirke point.

1942 Railway Cup winners.

Front row: *J. Barry, J. Lynch, W. O'Donnell (Capt.), D. Gorman, J. McCarthy, P. Cregan, J. Quirke.*

Back row: *J. Keane, D. Stokes, J. Ryan, W. Murphy, C. Ring, W. Barron, B. Thornhill, J. Power, C. Moylan.*

In 1942, it was Munster's turn to get the bye into the final and it was the old familiar line-up for the final when Leinster had a semi-final win by ten points over Connacht in Ballinasloe. This was the St Patrick's Day on which Ulster, captained by John Joe O'Reilly, and including greats like Alf Murray and Kevin Armstrong, won the football trophy for the first time after losing four previous finals. For Munster hurlers, though, it was a very different story: they were seeking the province's eleventh triumph before a crowd of 16,200 and within two minutes of the start they jumped into the lead when their captain, Tipperary's Bill O'Donnell, goaled from a free and soon Christy Ring added the first of his four points. Jack Lynch was in excellent form at midfield beside Christy Moylan of Waterford and he had two points in the first half, one of them from a 'seventy', before Munster edged into a half-time lead of 1-7 to 2-1. Early in the second half they substantially increased their lead with two goals by Limerick's Jackie Power, the second one set-up by Jack Lynch, and Jack added a point to leave the scores 3-8 to 2-3.

However, when it looked as if Munster might coast to victory they were hit by two sudden Leinster goals to which Jim Langton tacked on an equalising point and there was a most exciting finish. Christy Moylan was soon through for another Munster goal and Dick Stokes wrapped up the victory with a late point: 4-9 to 4-5.

1943

1943 Railway Cup winners.

Front row: *J. Quirke, J. Young, T. Doyle, C. Ring, J. Power, P. Cregan, J. Maher.*

Back row: *J. Keane, D. Stokes, B. Thornhill, W. O'Donnell, J. Lynch (Capt.), A. Fleming, M. Mackey, W. Murphy, J. Barry.*

When Munster went to Nenagh in February 1943 to play Connacht in the semi-final, Jack Lynch was honoured with the captaincy and he played a crucial role in the province's three-point win over the westerners. Consequently, he had the honour of leading out Munster on St Patrick's Day against the old rivals Leinster before 25,170, the biggest crowd so far at the finals. The referee for that hurling game was Dr Joe Stuart, who would be elected President of the Association 15 years later, and again, in a repeat of the previous year, a very early Munster goal by Bill O'Donnell opened the scoring after he took a long pass from Jack Lynch. Jim Langton suddenly made a huge impact on the game and he got a sequence of two goals and a point without reply from Munster to give Leinster a four-point lead at the interval. However, early in the second half Jack and Christy Ring added points for the south, Langton got another point but Jackie Power's goal left the scores level. Leinster took over again with two Kilkennymen restoring their lead: Langton 0-2 and Jimmy Walsh 1-1. The last quarter was played out in a welter of excitement and John Quirke and Jackie Power had goals to bring the scores level, before Christy Ring secured the all-important point that gave Munster a one-point victory 4-3 to 3-5. Jack Lynch mounted the steps of the old Hogan Stand to take away the trophy for the southern province.

Jack had now got a fifth medal in the blue jersey and his name entered the record books as a winning inter-provincial captain. Eleven months later he became even more famously enshrined in Railway Cup folklore when he played three matches on the same day, two of them the hurling and football semi-finals with Munster. That was February 20 1944, and at that time he was living in Dublin and playing with the Civil Service club, so before heading for Croke Park he turned out for the club before lunch in a morning senior league match. However, as he revealed in a radio interview nearly 40 years later, he most likely wouldn't have undertaken such a feat but for the lady he had married two years later.

'I was playing with Civil Service and doing a line with Máirín at the time,' he said, 'and when she asked me what I was going to do I said "I'll go to Croke Park, I don't think I'll play with Civil Service in the morning."

So, even though she wasn't a typical GAA person, she said, "Well, surely, your club must come first," and I said, "Goodness, you're right". So he went to Islandbridge for the league match against Eoghan Ruadh and the following day brought the headline 'Jack Lynch Had A Busy Day' over the news that he had scored in all three matches: a goal and a point for Civil Service, two points for Munster footballers and one in the hurling game. However, the story behind the headline wasn't disclosed.

Years later he reminisced: 'It was a funny saga in a way. I went out to Islandbridge and the Service selectors asked me if I was going to play. I said I would, but would they mind if I played in goal. They replied, 'No, but we might want you out the field later,' so I went into goal for the first half. Now five balls came my way, there were three goals, one a point and one wide, and I decided it was time to give up any aspirations I might have had to be a goalkeeper.' After moving outfield in the second half he contributed the 1-2, but that first half had been a disaster and Eoghan Ruadh had an easy victory.

There followed a hurried journey to the other side of the city. 'We had no track-suits and I just pulled up my trousers over the togs and put on a jacket and dashed to Croke Park, changed jerseys and got out with Munster in the hurling match, which we won easily against Ulster. I lined-out immediately for the football, against Ulster again, after changing jerseys – to change the number rather than the colour. I remember coming towards the end of the match, when I think we were a point or two down, and somebody passed the ball from the left corner to me. I had to run fairly fast to get it and I got near it, but I honestly hadn't the energy to kick it. It would have been an easy goal. After that I decided that I would never again play three matches in one day.' Munster lost that football game to the champions of the previous two years, so Jack wasn't faced with the prospect of playing in the two finals. He had nearly four weeks to recover before facing Connacht hurlers, who had shocked Leinster in the other semi-final at Birr. For more than half of that final it looked as if Connacht might do the same to Munster, they were still three years away from their initial hurling triumph. They led 2-4 to 2-3 in the opening minutes of the second half, Munster equalised shortly afterwards with a Seán Condon point and regained the lead with a Jack Lynch pointed free. Jack contributed more than his four points to the 4-10 to 4-4 victory according to one account which stated: 'Munster's big pull was at centrefield where Jack Lynch stood out on his own even with Pierce Thornton playing a topping game.' For most of the game Jack was partnered by his Glen Rovers' clubmate Christy Ring after switches sent Seán Condon, scorer of 1-2, forward.

1944

1944 Railway Cup winners.

Front row: *J. Power, C. Ring, J. Young, C. Cottrell.*

Centre row: *P.J. Quain, J. Quirke, S. Condon (Capt.), P. Cregan, W. Murphy, J. Barry.*

Back row: *J. Mackey, J. Lynch, D. Stokes, S. McCarthy, A. Fleming, J. Ware, B. Thornhill.*

Incidentally, the 1944 hurling semi-final which Munster won, marked Ulster's first appearance in the competition.

Even though war was still raging in Europe, and Ireland was suffering the deprivations of rationing and reduced transport, the crowds were increasing annually at the Railway Cup competitions. New records were set every St Patrick's Day and the attendance was up again in 1944 to 31,031 and continuing to grow.

For a time now, Jack Lynch's association with the Munster hurling team ceased and in a four-year period, 1945-48, he was not chosen even among the subs. All the more surprising, then, that he re-appeared in the blue jersey in February 1949. Although Cork had been dethroned the previous summer by Waterford, obviously Jack's form impressed the provincial selectors again, particularly the part he played in the National League final win over Tipperary in October 1948. He was over 31 years of age when listed fourth among the five subs announced by Munster on January 3, but was not called upon during the semi-final victory over Leinster six weeks later. The side for the final was named on March 7 and his name appeared second on the subs after Mick Hayes of Waterford. Even though he wasn't used as a replacement during the final on St Patrick's Day, Munster's 5-3 to 2-9 win before another record crowd (40,091) enabled him collect the seventh medal which is now on display in the Croke Park museum.

Some Cork people might expect Jack's collection of Railway Cup medals to include one for football because they may have read in some publications that he was associated with the 1946 team that won the interprovincial football competition by, first, beating Connacht in Cork and then, Leinster at Croke Park. It is true that he was actually named in the team for that particular competition when it was selected on December 1 1945. As confirmed recently by provincial secretary, Donie Nealon, from the council minutes, Jack, was not included on the hurling side, but was chosen at right full-forward for football, having filled that position less than three months before in the All-Ireland final against Cavan. However, he never got to wear the blue jersey that year – and therein lies a tale.

The first inkling Cork supporters got that something was amiss most likely came from rumour around the city, if not further afield in the county.

Certainly, they weren't informed by the newspapers of the day; information was sparse. For example, reading reports of the February 10 Cork win over Kilkenny in Nowlan Park which gave the county group honours in the National Hurling League, followers must have wondered why two stalwarts, Jack Lynch and Paddy O'Donovan, weren't listed in the team. Three days later they were a little wiser when they perused the short *Cork Examiner* report of the weekly county board meeting. After Mr Tom O'Reilly of the hurling selection committee reported on the team 'earning a well-deserved victory' in the first outing of the year, the county chairman, William Walsh, stated that there had been some controversy as to why two players were not selected for the game. He added that he had since satisfied himself that the selection committee had been quite right in not selecting these players. 'The two of them had automatically suspended themselves,' he said. As was the practice of the time, particularly when there was a hint of controversy, and in sharp contrast to present day more informative reportage, the account of the meeting contained no names and readers were not told how the unnamed players had 'automatically suspended themselves'.

Of course, soon afterwards Cork folk learned that these two great players had been reported to the county board for attending a rugby match at the Mardyke on January 12. Under the Ban rules they had to serve a suspension of at least three months from the date of what colleague, Edmund Van Esbeck, tells me was the only Irish final trial ever held outside Dublin. Jack Lynch had a particular interest in the game as his brother-in-law, John Harvey, the UCC and Munster full back, was playing for the Rest team against the Probables.

The Railway Cup football semi-final against Connacht was due on February 24 and in previewing the game the *Irish Independent* declared: '...at least one new forward will have to be found to replace J. Lynch (Cork),' and *The Cork Examiner* referred to 'the dropping of J. Lynch from the team'. As expected, on the Sunday, the selectors called Seán Cleary of Tipperary from the subs to play at right corner-forward. Munster won 1-6 to 0-5, but when the team for the final was announced early in March, Cleary was relegated again and a reshuffled full-forward line saw Dan Kavanagh

(Kerry) moved from half forward. E. 'Togher' Casey of Cork was named as left full, but he cried-off a few days before the final and it was Jackie Lyne of Kerry who filled the position against Leinster. It was only the fourth football triumph for Munster – a win firmly founded on the midfield superiority of Cork's Eamonn Young and Tipperary's Mick Cahill, whose great talents were well known to those of us who shared schooldays with him at Knockbeg College, Carlow, a few years earlier.

Before that final, however, nobody was in any doubt as to why Lynch and Donovan were out of action. It had been reported that Cork were notified by the secretary of the Munster Council, Seán McCarthy, that the players were appealing against the ruling of the county chairman on February 12 that they were automatically suspended under Rule 13, page 39. They appealed, they said, because they 'were charged with no particular offence, were not given the opportunity to appear in our own defence and the chairman was not in possession of sufficient evidence on which to base his charge'. Within days Jack and Paddy changed their minds and on February 28 the papers revealed that 'they had withdrawn their appeal to the Munster Council against their suspension under the "foreign games" rule.'

So they served out their sentence, which ended just in time to allow them return to the Cork hurling team for the National League semi-final at Croke Park on April 7, which Dublin won easily. They were again firmly re-established as key players in the side by the summer of that year when they would both contribute with distinction to Cork's memorable campaign for the recapture of the All-Ireland championship. That culminated with the victory over Kilkenny in September – an occasion that brought Jack Lynch his historic sixth successive All-Ireland medal. Consequently, the disappointment of missing the interprovincial football medal in the spring was well and truly banished.

12

The National Hurling League

THE NATIONAL HURLING league was organised for the first time in 1925–26 and Cork were the initial winners of the title, defeating Dublin in the final. Cork again beat Dublin in the 1929–30 decider. Jack Lynch made his first appearance in a final in the 1936–37 competition when Cork lost to Limerick, but was back as captain in 1939–40 when Cork defeated Tipperary. He figured again in 1940–41 when Dublin were once more defeated.

Toss of the coin at Cork vs Kilkenny, National Hurling League, 22 October 1939.

Jack Lynch and Jimmy Walsh await the outcome watched by the referee Mick Fitzgibbon, Willie Campbell and Christy Ring who was playing his first senior game with Cork.

The league was suspended due to travel restrictions from 1942 to 1945. Cork's next title came in 1948 when, under the captaincy of Jim Young. They defeated Tipperary on the score of 3-3 to 1-2, but the result was reversed in the following year's final with Tipperary winning by two points, 3-5 to 3-3.

1939–40 and 1940–41 National league winners.

Front row: *J. Quirke, C. Ring, W. Campbell.*

Centre row: *D.J. Buckley, B. Ryng, J. Barrett, T. O'Sullivan, M. Brennan.*

Back row: *B. Thornhill, C. Buckley, J. Lynch (Capt.), W. Murphy, A. Lotty, J. Young, J. Buttimer, J. Barry.*

Jack Lynch played in five finals, and following his display in the 1948 decider was on the Munster team selection for the 1949 Railway Cup. He was always available for league games and one of the county's outstanding players down through the years. This was especially so in the 1948–49 play-off against Kilkenny.

1948

1948 NATIONAL HURLING LEAGUE FINAL

Jack Lynch excels in Cork's league play-off victory

Cork gave a grand display and their performance put them right back in the line of favourites for the 1949 championship honours. In the first half, it was the Cork forwards who were the outstanding unit on the field. Jack Lynch was at the peak of his form, and was the most prolific scorer of the match, one goal and six points coming from his hurley with apparent ease. His strength was a great asset in the half-forward line, and added to that, he was in rare shooting form, many of his points being scored from difficult angles while he was actually hard pressed by several black and amber defenders.

Cork vs Tipperary at Croke Park.

Jim Young leads out the Cork team followed by Willie Murphy, Jack Lynch, Tom Mulcahy, Willie John Daly, Paddy O'Donovan, Mick O'Toole, Bernie Murphy, Donie Twomey, Joe Hartnett. Tipperary players include Tommy Doyle, Tommy Purcell, Tony Reddin.

**1948, Jack Lynch kicks the sliotar over the bar despite losing his hurley.
Jim Devitt (Tipperary) comes in to challenge.**

Jack's last league final was against Tipperary in the 1949 final which Cork lost by two points after a thrilling encounter. He won three National League medals to add to his championship victories.

Off the Field

A Helicopter trip over Lough Foyle, Derry.

Páirc an Chrócaigh.

cumann lúit cleas gaedeal
Clár Oifigeamail (Official Programme) Luac 2d.

What a pride and glory it is to witness the stirring scenes associated with a well-played, cleanly and keenly contested Gaelic match, especially in Hurling; to feel the thrills coursing through one's veins as the springy ash Camans crash in the air above and on the sod below; and to realise that here is being enacted before our excited and admiring gaze, a vivid symbol of the long ago; a sure reminder that Knocknagow is not dead; and a striking and soul-stirring guarantee that by Shannon, Suir and Lee, and by hillside and glenside throughout the province, the virile manhood and traditions of our race are keeping a firm hold on their hard-won inheritance.

Seán Mac Cárταιξ, b.e., Chairman, at Munster Convention, 1940

1940
munster
Championship
REPLAY

SENIOR HURLING

AT THURLES
SUNDAY, AUGUST 4th, 1940

SENIOR HURLING FINAL REPLAY

corcaiξ   v.   Luimneac
(CORK)   (LIMERICK)

3.45 p.m., Summer Time.   Referee—D. Ryan, Kerry.

ALL-IRELAND JUNIOR FOOTBALL SEMI-FINAL—WESTMEATH v. CORK

Admission to Field · 1s.; Stand (1s.), Sideline (2s.) extra

Rúnaróe

LEINSTER LEADER, LTD., NAAS

With Jackie Kennedy.

At the Curragh races.

Jack reading in his office.

With Máirín relaxing at Buncrana,
County Donegal.

Giving King Boudouin
of Belgium some tips,
watched by Seán Ó
Siocháin and President
de Valera.

13

From the Homes of Tipperary

Pat Stakelum, captain of Tipperary's All-Ireland winning team of 1949 and one of the stars of their three-in-a-row victories of 1949, '50, and '51 recalls:

> Growing up in the forties around Holycross and Thurles, the name of Jack Lynch would always be mentioned when any discussion took place on hurling. We had the greatest respect at all times for his ability to dominate and dictate the play. Coming on to the Tipperary team in 1949 brought me up against him and I vividly remember his amazing goal in the first match which brought Cork back into the game.
>
> In our home and in the homes of Tipperary, his name evoked memories of great clashes in which victory or defeat were accepted in a sportsmanlike manner. He never forgot his hurling days and always made time to seek out and reminisce with old team-mates and opponents alike.
>
> In 1975, I was captain of the Hurler's Golfing Society and I invited Jack, Mick Mackey and some other retired hurlers to play on my prize day. What an honour it was for me when they came along to play! Jack stayed on for the celebrations which completed a memorable day for me.

Cork vs Tipperary, 1942 Munster final.

Jack Lynch leads out the team followed by Mick Kennefick, Paddy O'Donovan, Jim Young, Ned Porter, Derry Beckett, Christy Ring, John Quirke and the rest of the team.

When Paddy Leahy, the Tipperary hurling 'supremo' of the '40s and '50s was seriously ill in Mount Carmel Hospital in Dublin in 1965, Jack was a regular visitor. I happened to be present when he called in one evening and during the conversation, Paddy took issue with Jack about his views on the 'Ban' rule.

'I see you're in favour of removing the "Ban" Jack,' says Paddy.

'I think it would benefit the association greatly if we got rid of it,' says Jack.

'If we get rid of it, we will be playing into the hands of those who would like to see the association split,' says Paddy.

'Gosh, I never thought of it that way Paddy,' replied Jack.

A very human response which would not offend his friend.

Séamus Ó Riain, of Moneygall, Tipperary, President of Cumann Lúthchleas Gael 1967-69, recalls an unexpected visit:

On Easter Sunday, 1967, I was elected President of the GAA. It was an honour and a responsibility that I greatly appreciated. On the following Wednesday some friends had gathered in our home to express their congratulations. The doorbell rang and when I answered the call, John O'Dea, who was Jack's driver, informed me that the Taoiseach wished to see me. Accompanied by his wife, Máirín, he came forward with an outstretched hand to offer his congratulations and best wishes. He came in and greeted my wife, Mary, and all present, sat down around the fire and we had a very enjoyable and pleasant evening.

The visit was a typical response by Jack Lynch. He considered it important to leave aside the calls and burdens of the head of Government, to call to our village, seek out our house and convey his good wishes to me for a successful term as head of an association he held in high regard.

I shall always cherish that happy memory of Jack's visit, a man of the people.

14

Spirit of the Glen

An article written by Jack for the Glen Rovers' history,
Spirit of the Glen, **1973**

'MY EARLIEST KNOWLEDGE of Glen Rovers was when I was a very small boy attending a match they played against St Anne's at Intermediate grade in the Mardyke on a fine Friday evening in summer. There were many matches played in those years, the 1920s, between the Glen and St Anne's. The rivalry was often very keen and, as often happens in such cases, that rivalry led to a very happy association that enhanced the quality and fame of hurling north of the Lee.

It would be difficult to chronicle the many incidents of my association with the Glen ranging back over almost half a century. I remember the many lemonade parties we had in Paddy O'Connell's house in Walsh's Avenue and the old St Nicks' clubroom in Wherland's Lane celebrating victories in juvenile and minor grades, the socials in the old Glen clubroom in Bird's Quay, mending hurleys under the keen eye of Capper Mullins in the old lean-to shed behind the clubroom in which many a good Glen team was selected.

There were, of course, highlights – our weekend 'tours' to play matches in places like Grenagh and Ballincollig when our modes of conveyance varied between lorries and bikes. My first junior hurling game with the Glen was when I was about 12 or 13 against Fr Mathew Hall in the City Junior Championship. The Glen were short a man and I was pushed in 'at the deep end'. The only other man present who could have played was Paddy O'Connell and he, as a senior player, was ineligible. I think I am correct when I say that Mick Casey, later to be one of the Glen's best goalies, played against us that day.

My first senior match was in the semi-final of the Championship in 1934 played against Seandún at the Mardyke. The late Josa Lee, our captain, had suffered a recurrence of his knee cartilage injury which plagued his entire hurling career. I was picked as his replacement. I had got my chance but I hopelessly fluffed it and though we won the match I contributed very little. The following day I was summoned to the 'presence' of 'The Ceann', the late Billy Connor. Our chairman's 'pet title' derived from the office of Ceann Comhairle of Dáil Éireann. I did not appreciate at the time that swimming and field games did not go very well together. 'Young man,' Billy said, 'I am given to understand that you were swimming every day before this important championship game.' 'I was,' I answered, 'the weather was so fine.' 'I thought so,' was the reply, 'your play had all the appearance of it. Don't let it happen again.' That was the end of the interview and the end of any swimming while training for important matches, such was the discipline enforced by our then beloved chairman.

My first Senior Inter-County game was in the 1935 League campaign. The Glen, as County champions, took the selection of the County team. We played Limerick in the Park and I was marking John Mackey, then at the height of his fame. I did reasonably well against him. I remember one instance when we were both running for a ball, I suddenly sprawled on the ground writhing in pain. I was, at the time, prone to cramps in the calf of my leg. Some of my colleagues assumed that John Mackey had done something to me and they were about to take a course of action that they thought would be appropriate. I shouted, 'He did nothing to me – it's a cramp!' I recall this incident here because I want to put on record that in many a subsequent tussle with John Mackey I found him to be a fair, though tough, opponent.

My first game in the Munster Championship was in the first round against Clare in Thurles in 1936. After a drawn game we re-played in Limerick. I remember it was a wet day and Clare beat us by a cricket score. Not a good outcome for the Glen selection and I felt that I would never see an All-Ireland medal.

Indeed, Cork's championship record in the remainder of the '30s did little to raise my hopes. Worse still for my club colleagues and myself on these Cork teams, Glen Rovers were County Champions during these years and proud as we were to bring the County Championship Cup 'across the River' for the first time in 1934, the assertion that Cork would not win an All-Ireland until the Cup re-crossed the river made us all the more despondent. We were rather surprisingly beaten by Waterford in the Munster Championship in 1938. We lost the 1939 All-Ireland 'Thunder & Lightning Final' to Kilkenny by the traditional point. You can imagine our joy and satisfaction at seeing the break-through come in 1941, when 'Sonny' Buckley, the Glen captain, led Cork to victory ten years after the famous 1931 three-game final. Incidentally, Paddy O'Connell – the Father of the Glen – brought me to see the first of these matches, the first time I was in Croke Park. The prominent part played by Glen members in the successive All-Ireland victories of the '40s and the '50s was great recompense for the lean years of the '30s.

There was an incident which has nothing to do with hurling but which I think is worth recording. One late December evening in the early years of the Second World War, I visited the old club room in Bird's Quay where about 12 of the members, mostly playing members, were at a game of cards around the fire. Towards teatime the card game ended and conversation developed. One former member, back home for Christmas from England where he had been working for a number of years, started to tell a mildly 'smutty' story. To a man, all the other members rose and started to hit him on the head with the soft part of their peak caps. A gentle but most salutary demonstration of what would not be tolerated in the precincts of the Glen Rovers Club.

Glen Rovers' Building Committee in 1953.

Front row: *T. Logue, J.C. Barry, Rev. Dr Harte, J. Lynch, S. O'Connell.*

Back Row: *Seamus O'Brien, Seán O'Brien, J. Lyons, J. Lynam, D. O'Donovan.*

In September 1936, I took a temporary job in Dublin while awaiting the outcome of a number of State examinations that I sat for in my final year at school. A few days before I came home for Christmas holidays I learned from the Civil Service Commission that my appointment to the Civil Service was imminent. As it happened, it took effect on 29 December and to my great joy I was assigned to the Circuit Court Office in Cork. A couple of days before that, I was in the rooms following a bout of hurling 'up the field' and Paddy 'Fox' Collins who was as efficient a Secretary of the Club as he was a hurler, asked me when I was going to Dublin. Apparently, the intention was to make me a presentation. I said I was not going back as I had just been assigned to Cork. He produced a case from his pocket in which was a new wristwatch. 'What will I do with this so?' he asked. 'It's already suitably inscribed, so you may as well have it.' Naturally, I gratefully accepted it. This little incident shows the thoughtfulness of Glen Rovers for their players.

Arriving for the opening of the extension to the Glen Rovers club in 1970.

I have not attempted in this article to chronicle names or games. There have been so many great people in the Glen, whether as players or background workers, whom it has been my privilege to be associated with and it would take many articles this size to write adequately about them. It in no way detracts from great clubs like the Barrs, Blackrock or Sarsfields, if I say that modern hurling not only in Cork, but throughout the country, owes much to Glen Rovers. The club members and supporters have shown, over the years, an unsurpassed loyalty and dedication to their club, their county and to the great game of hurling. A practical example of this is that they were the first club, I think, in the GAA to recognise the needs of modern youth if they were to be held for GAA games, and to take positive steps to provide for these needs. In the early '50s it was seen that young lads were not coming forward to show a practical interest in the games in the same numbers as in previous years. The Glen decided that indoor amenities should be provided so that activities like basketball, etc., could be pursued, especially during the winter evenings.

**Glen Rovers and Mount Sion teams with Jack at the opening of
Glen Rovers' field, July 1971.**

A committee was set up of which Rev. Dr S. Harte was chairman, and on which old members like T. Logue (Snr) and S. O'Connell served with some younger members. The deliberations were quick and decisive – borrow the money from the bank, erect the hall and pay off the debt through bazaars, bingo, etc., which would be run in the hall. The Glen have set a very good and necessary example.'

15

Jack's Dublin Connection

**An article written by Jack for *The Civil
Service GAA Club History* by Tom Woulfe**

'I HAD PLAYED with the Cork footballers for a few years before 1943, the
year we got as far as the All-Ireland semi-final when Cavan beat us. I
honestly thought that this was the end of my entire inter-county football
career, having left Cork that autumn to pursue my Bar lectures in Dublin.

I have always maintained that no matter how many championships you
win, you wouldn't win any unless you played with a good team. The Civil
Service football team that I played with was a good team. The quality of men
like Jack and Bertie Murphy, Frank Dowling, Mick Falvey, Seán McCarthy,
John Joe Maher and Alec Tansey rubbed off on one, and favourable reports
of my contribution percolated down to Cork during the course of the
Dublin senior championship. So, instead of being forgotten by the Cork
football selectors, I was lucky enough to get my place on another good team,
the Cork 1945 team, and won an All-Ireland football medal.

People will say of any sporting activity that winning is not everything;
participation is what is important. I certainly enjoyed my two seasons with
Civil Service in 1944–45, playing with a quality team against quality teams,
and the satisfaction of winning a Dublin senior championship medal was
an added bonus.

The quality of 'service' was not only on the pitch, but on the sidelines as
well. The team was well and enthusiastically managed and instructed by
men like Paddy Kerins and Tom Woulfe. It was a great lesson for me, having

been born into the GAA and bred in a parochial school-cum-club environment, to be thrust into a group of disparate people who, because of their vocational *esprit de corps* and commitment to Gaelic games were able to instil into such a heterogeneous bunch of fellows, the will, the cohesion and pride to win the championship of a county, in which, especially the football, was hardest won.'

1944

EVENING HERALD

DUBLIN COUNTY FOOTBALL FINAL

Honours for Civil Service

Civil Service 3–4   **Peadar Mackens 1–1**

Making their first appearance in a Dublin championship final, Civil Service footballers won readily from Peadar Mackens at Croke Park yesterday. A half-time switch that brought Bertie Murphy back from full forward to centre forward played a great part in securing Civil Service their first Dublin senior football title on the score of 3-4 to 1-1. The backs did their work splendidly in the first half, when they were well tested. Dowling and Lynch were outstanding, while O'Mahony, Moore and O'Shea ably helped to link defence and midfield.

Peadar Macken's were well served by P. Kennedy as the keystone. Bolger, Driver, O'Sullivan, John Delaney, and Foley played splendidly.

The Civil Service Team, which contained players from ten counties, lined out as follows:

J. Thornton (Louth), D. Foley (Cork), F. Dowling, captain (Kildare),
J. Lynch (Cork), S. O'Mahony (Waterford), T. Moore (Kerry),
S. O'Shea (Cork), Alec Tansey (Sligo), S. McCarthy (Kerry),
B. Maguire (Leitrim), M. Falvey (Kerry), J.J. Maher,(Tipperary),
J. Maguire (Meath), B. Murphy (Kerry), A. Halpin (Dublin).

Civil Service Team Photo at Croke Park, October 1 1944.

(Bertie Murphy missing)

Front row: *J. Lynch, S. O'Shea, A. Tansey, J. Maguire, S. Thornton, D. Kinnane, S. O'Mahony, J.J. Maher.*

Back row: *F. Dowling (Capt.), S. Dooney, A. Halpin, M. Falvey, J. McGroarty, B. Maguire, T. Moore, S. McCarthy.*

16

Travels With Jack

John O'Dea

J OHN O'DEA from Kildorrery, County Cork, was Jack Lynch's official
driver, and security person from September 1960 to September 1993.
Tom O'Loughlin from Clare shared the same duties with him for 25
years.

Tom and myself had the great privilege of working with Jack Lynch for
many years. We travelled with him throughout the country and overseas to
many functions. Of course, the biggest bonus we had was the opportunity
to attend so many GAA games in which both of us had a great interest.

If there was any hint of a game on as we passed through a town or village,
and we had time on our hands, Jack would stop to have a peep. A favourite
spot was Riverstown, on the way into Cork, the home of the Sarsfields club.
If there was a game on, 'Micka' Brennan would be there and many great
battles would be recalled.

Going to the major games was a great day out for us. Jack always ensured
that we had a first-class view of the action and we would have a great
discussion on the game on our journey home. What fascinated me was the
recall he had of seemingly minor events which took place during the game,
and how he could point out what bearing these had on the result.

1977, Munster final in Thurles, Cork vs Clare.

He would never show emotion during a game especially when Cork or the Glen were playing, but if they were victorious he would always be so overjoyed and happy.

He loved going to Thurles. It was his favourite venue and the best field in the country for hurling. 'If you were not able to play hurling in Thurles, you couldn't play it anywhere,' he used to say.

Mrs Lynch would nearly always accompany us to the games and we used to stop in Tipperary at a lay-by near Cahir for our picnic. On one occasion Bishop Lucey of Cork travelled with us back to Dublin, after a Munster final in Cork. He was flying out to Rome the next morning. He organised a picnic basket from the nuns in a convent in Montennotte which we duly collected and we stopped at our usual spot outside of Cahir. Everything was perfect until it was discovered that no knife was included to butter the bread. After some deliberations on how to overcome the problem, Jack pulled out a nail-file, sterilised it with boiling water, and proceeded to butter the bread for the sandwiches.

I played quite a lot of hurling with my home club Kildorrery and was always facilitated to do so. On one famous occasion, I was playing with my divisional team, Avondhu, against the Glen in the senior hurling championship at Fermoy. The Glen won but I received a fairly serious head injury and I was removed to hospital to be treated. Jack had engagements in Cork that evening to which he drove himself. The next morning he came out to Kildorrery to collect me and drove to Dublin.

He always had great respect and time for former hurlers, colleagues or opponents alike. When in Limerick, he regularly called to see John Mackey who was seriously ill for a number of years and when in Kilkenny he always gave Paddy Grace a call.

Those of us who worked with Jack Lynch over the years will always remember the respect and generosity which both he and Mrs Lynch bestowed on us at all times. When Tom retired, a farewell party was held in their own house and on the silver jubilee of my wedding, Mrs Lynch organised a surprise party for my wife and myself at Springfort Hall outside Mallow to which our relations and friends were all invited.

Great times and great memories.

**Jack, Máirín, John O'Dea, Angela O'Dea,
Bridie O'Loughlin and Tom O'Loughlin.**

17
Those Were The Days

**Article written by Jack for the Official
Opening of Pairc Uí Chaoimh, 1976**

'It is strange that my very first memory of the Cork Athletic Grounds is as a potential athlete, an athlete in the sense of sports rather than field games. It was as a competitor in the Cork City Primary Schools' Sports in the late twenties. In fact, it was then I won my first medal, as it happened a bronze one, in the Under-12 100-yards dash.

My next most vivid memory was perhaps in 1930 when the Glen took part in their first senior county championship final when they lost to Blackrock. We left Blackpool that day with high hopes and although they were dashed, the disappointment I felt at the end of that day quickly disappeared as I felt that success was sure to come, if not the following year, then very soon after it. The Glen had a big reservoir of talent building up in their very successful minor teams under the tutelage of Paddy O'Connell around that period. It was under Paddy's 'wing' that I came to that 1930 final. In fact, he pulled me into the pre-match picture of the team, a picture that is now part of the lore of Glen Rovers. And of course success did come – we won our first of the eight-in-a-row in 1934. As in 1930 I watched that final also from the side-line, as a sub, although I had played, not too well I am afraid, in the semi-final against Seandun as a replacement for one of the regulars who was injured.

Cork's hurling final in 1971, Blackrock vs St Finbarrs at the old Cork Athletic Grounds. Máirín Lynch and Jack accompanied by Jack Barrett, chairman of the Cork County Board.

It is very difficult to recount in any detail all the subsequent finals I played in without access to the newspaper records. We did have some titanic struggles against the Barrs, Ballincollig, Carrigtwohill on one occasion, and Blackrock.

Perhaps the matches against the Barrs will be the most vivid in my memory, firstly, because it was the Barrs that the Glen beat in their first final victory of 1934 and it was against the Barrs that we had our most thrilling struggles in the years that followed. I well remember the tension that seemed to grip most of the city during the pre-match days. One could almost feel the tension in the atmosphere as one used to do in the square of Thurles prior to a Munster hurling final. It was little wonder that with the interest that these games evoked, it was not unusual for about 30,000 people to attend these finals.

Connie Buckley leads out the Glen team prior to the 1941 County final against Ballincollig at the old Cork Athletic Grounds.

It would be smug of me not to recall games in which the Glen were on the losing side – for example, the day in 1942 when Ballincollig brought our eight-in-a-row run to an end, or on a day in 1946 when atrocious conditions, similar to those I will refer to later, obtained. The Barrs were a point or so ahead in the last few minutes. There was a mêlée in the mud in front of the Barrs goal. The ball was not even visible. I fell on the ground and found the ball in my hand. Through a small misdemeanour, I got it over the goal line but Con Murphy, who refereed the game and who has played such a prominent part in providing the magnificent Páirc Uí Chaoimh, spotted it and quite rightly, although to my annoyance at the time, disallowed the goal. The final whistle came seconds later. And so Seán Condon, Mick Kennefick and company heralded a new era for the Barrs.

In those years Ballincollig's great efforts certainly merited a county title. No one would have begrudged Willie Murphy a county medal as no one begrudged Micka Brennan his medal in 1951, when Sarsfields won their first county title after a long, long wait. It was former Glen Rover, Pat O'Leary, who captained the winning Sarsfields team on that occasion against his old team. We did not begrudge him his success either: after all, had he not married or was then courting Alan Lotty's sister. I think Seán O'Brien, who captained the Glen on that day expressed the feelings of us all, when he walked the full length of the field to the city-end dressing room to congratulate Sarsfields on their historic win. Incidentally it was the Glen who were on the losing side in 1956 when Blackrock re-emerged as county champions and as a force again in the county hurling scene.

My first inter-county experience in the Park was, I think, in 1933 when I was a member of the Cork minor hurling team in the final against Tipperary. Tipp under the guidance of the late and great Johnny Leahy, dominated the minor inter-county hurling scene during those years. There was no limit on the number of subs that could be introduced on a team. Johnny Leahy invariably used six or seven and the striking thing was that each sub who came on seemed to be a better performer than any player already on the field. Needless to mention, the wiles and guiles of Tipp and Johnny Leahy beat us on that day also. From the senior inter-county hurling point of view I hope I will be forgiven if I recall as my most abiding memory the 1942 Munster Hurling Final when we beat Tipp and beat them very well. It was during the four-in-a-row series and was the year in which I had the honour of captaining an All-Ireland winning team. Many years later, Paddy Leahy, brother of Johnny whom I have mentioned earlier admitted to me that this was one of the greatest surprises that Tipperary encountered during his period in charge of the team. I remember it particularly for the battle royal that Paddy O'Donovan and I had at mid-field against Jimmy Cooney and Bill O'Donnell. Leahy told me that they expected that this pair, already well established, could on their own beat Cork, but O'Donovan and I managed to hold them and I think had a little to spare. Suffice it to say that our forwards were able to get plenty of the ball and made good use of it. Christy Ring scored several points on that day mainly from the service he got from midfield.

My outstanding football memory of the old Cork Athletic Grounds was the Munster football final of 1943 in which we played against Kerry. Kerry had all the stars on that occasion – Paddy Bán Brosnan, Paddy Kennedy, Joe Keohane, etc. It was a very wet day and that perhaps assisted us in beating what probably was a much better football side than ours on that occasion. During one phase of the play, I remember running for a ball with Paddy Bán Brosnan and it was clear that whoever would stay on his feet was likely to win the ball. So, at a crucial stage I caught Paddy on the wrong foot and nudged him with my right shoulder. Paddy came down and literally slithered across the slippery surface and ended up wedged between the grass and one of the low front sideline seats which were only about a foot off the ground. Paddy actually had to be pulled out of his embarrassing posture. Great sportsman that he was, he showed not the slightest rancour.

Strangely enough, it was another wet day that calls forth my next memory. It was on a Tuesday in late August, 1942. We were training for the All-Ireland final and with the field in a quagmire and a driving south-westerly rain-laden wind, Jim Barry was in two minds whether to put the team out training or not. Most of the city resident members of the team had arrived on their bikes but when the East Cork car with Bill Campbell and company, and then Con Cottrell from the South-East and Batt Thornhill arrived from North Cork, Jim decided to let us have a knock-about for about half an hour. Needless to mention when we came in we were covered in mud from head to foot and this brings into focus the contrast between the magnificent conditions that now pertain compared with those days. As usual we togged off under the old stand and in those days it was not partitioned as it had been in the last 20 years or so of its life. There was an earthen floor and the seats consisted of timber planks laid on upturned butter boxes. We hung our clothes from nails driven into the serrated seats of the stand. The driving rain into the stand had caused the water to seep through the crevices and chinks and on to our clothes with the result that these were sodden when we arrived back after our short bout of training. We tried to clean the mud off ourselves from the one tap which supplied the water from a corner of the 'dressing room' area. In no time of course the water from the running tap turned the ground around it into a morass with the result that we could neither wash or dry ourselves.

Having retired early from our training session I had time to get to the County Board before the usual Tuesday night meeting had ended. At the request of the players I lodged a complaint about the conditions under which we were expected to train. I am afraid I got short shrift from the members of the County Board but I hope that the protest from the players that I conveyed helped in some way to provide the modest improvements which players of subsequent generations were able to enjoy. Nobody is more delighted than I, and my colleagues of those days, that now we have in Cork a stadium and facilities which are as good as may be found in any part of the world. *Gúim rath Dé ar an obair.*'

18

He Had No Peer

**Lynch's Graveside Oration
at Christy Ring's Funeral, March 1979**

'**B**EFORE WE LEAVE this hallowed spot let us bide just a few moments longer and cast our thoughts back over the years through which so many of us had the honour to know, to play with or against, Christy Ring. What more can be said of him, of his prowess, of his competitiveness that has not already been said?

**Jack presenting
Christy Ring with
his Hall of Fame
award in 1971.**

But more and more will be said and written of him as long as young men will match their hurling skills against each other on Ireland's green fields, as long as young boys swing their camáns for the sheer thrill of the tingle in their fingers of the impact of ash on leather, as long as hurling is played, the story of Christy Ring will be told – and that will be forever.

As long as the red jerseys of Cork and the blue of Munster and the green, black and gold of Glen Rovers, colours that Christy wore with such distinction, as long as we see these colours in manly combat, the memories of Christy's genius and prowess will come tumbling back with profusion.

We will relish and savour them, for we will hardly see their likes again. And men who are fathers and grandfathers now will tell their children and grandchildren with pride that they saw Christy Ring play. The story will pass from generation to generation and so it will live.

Even before half of his playing days were over, his feats and his skills were legendary. These inherent skills were enhanced by his sheer dedication to the game of hurling that he loved, and by his constant aspiring to improve his playing of it – if, indeed, that were possible.

As a hurler he had no peer. As a friend he was intensely loyal. As a man

At the unveiling of the Christy Ring monument at Cloyne in May, 1983. Jack Lynch with Mrs Rita Ring.

he was vibrant, intelligent and purposeful. As a husband and a father he was loving, concerned and tender. This I know.

All of you have come with him on this last journey, as he reaches his final Goal, his friends, his admirers, old hurlers who played with and against him; on behalf of Glen Rovers and St Nicholas clubs and, may I presume, on behalf of the Cork County Board; on behalf of Rita, young Christy and Mary, may I offer thanks and appreciation.'

JACK LYNCH
21, GARVILLE AVENUE,
RATHGAR,
DUBLIN 6.

4th May 1983

Mr Liam Ó Tuama,
1 Ballineaspaig Lawn
Bishopstown, Cork

Dear Liam,

Máirín and I would like to thank you and Coiste Cumhneacháin Criostóir Ó Rinn for your warm and generous hospitality last Sunday in Cloyne.

The unveiling ceremony was indeed an historic occasion and a tremendous success. I know well the tremendous amount of work that you personally, Dr McCarthy and the other members of the Committee put into it. It required enormous organisation and no detail no matter how small was overlooked. We would like to congratulate you all heartily on its success.

Finally, the Sculptured bronze of Christy Ring was excellent - everyone I met had nothing but praise for it. You certainly made a good choice in selecting Jan Zoulet to execute it.

Yours sincerely
Jack Lynch

Letter sent by Jack Lynch to Liam Ó Tuama after the unveiling of the Christy Ring monument.

19

To Wet My Old Whistle
With Porter

**Jack Lynch's speech at the opening of the Ballinascarthy
(County Cork) GAA grounds on Sunday, 29 May, 1983**

*One evening of late into Bandon I strayed
Bound for Clonakilty I straight made my way
At Ballinscarthy I some time delayed
To wet my old whistle with porter.*

*I scarcely had travelled a mile of the road
When I heard a dispute at a farmer's abode
'Twas the son of a landlord, an ill-looking toad
And the wife of a bold tenant farmer*

'THE WANDERING BARD goes on to tell us how the brave lady defied the landlord's son until "he showed us his heels and like lightning he flew". It illustrates how the hardy small tenant farmers of Ballinscarthy, under the banner of the Land League, refused to be cowed by greedy landlords. They who loved the land and cherished their heritage, were the forebears of those who now comprise the membership of Ballinascarthy GAA Club and who, in turn, equally cherish their heritage especially in the form of Gaelic games.

Opening of Ballinascarthy field, 1983.

Jack with club officers Leo Meade and Dan Holland. Louise O'Flynn looks on.

The Ballinascarthy Club was founded in 1945 and played their first game on a field which was once the property of the Ford family. It is believed that the forebears of the great Henry Ford settled in the Ballinascarthy area in the sixteenth century, but the first record of the Ford family tree dates from the middle of the eighteenth century. John Ford's grandfather was also a tenant farmer – probably a small one – as he left Ireland at the height of the Great Famine with his wife and seven sons, one of whom was William. Around 1860, William married the adopted daughter of another Corkman, Patrick Ahern, who had emigrated to America in 1825.

An extract from the personal diary of Henry Ford 1st reads: 'My grandfather was my mother's foster father. He was born in Cork City, Ireland, on March 17, 1804. He came to this country in about 1825. He and my grandmother lived with my parents. She died in 1871 and he in 1881. I do not remember her very well but I spent many happy days with him; when I was in Ireland in 1912, we went to the church in Cork and found the record of his birth. His name was Ahern. Her name, Margaret McGinn. My mother's name was Mary Litigot. My father's, William Ford.'

Henry Ford named his home in Dearborn, Michigan, 'Fair Lane' after his grandfather's birthplace – now Wolfe Tone Street – in Cork City. The name 'Fairlane' was also given to some of Ford's most successful car models.

But the Ford paternal line came from Ballinascarthy. So Ballinascarthy's sons showed their calibre and resilience in holding on to their land in the old country on the one hand and on the other hand, in the new world, showed their enterprise and initiative that revolutionised modern transport and work on the land.

The initiative and enterprise of this small club are most commendable, drawing its support from literally half of a small parish; they are now the proud owners of a well-equipped playing field and pavilion.

The club's record in the relatively short time since its foundation is also commendable. They have won a number of Cork South-West Divisional championships and can now field no less than 14 teams in different grades. Many long-established city clubs could well envy this progress.

In congratulating them on their achievement, I wish them further success in all their endeavours in the future and I thank them for giving me the honour of performing this formal opening in this historic location.'

20

The Lads And The Chaps

Jack Lynch's contribution for
Muskerry Golf History **by Tim O'Brien, 1985**

'I have very many happy memories of my membership of Muskerry, even if the quality of my golf did not contribute to them. I first joined the club in the early 1950s just before I ceased my other sporting activities, hurling and football. As in the case of many of my friends, that great and loyal Muskerry man, Frank Casey, initially invited me to become a member. I was already a member of the Dáil, and because of the job I had, was obliged to reside in Dublin.

I well remember how I looked forward to coming to Cork at weekends and especially when I had finished my 'clinic'. I used to have an appointment with Frank, Paddy O'Donovan, and Jim Murray for an afternoon of football. On many an occasion, I kept them waiting as a result of the number of people I had to meet, but they were always very patient and indulgent with me.

In the middle of the late '50s, a recurrence of an old hurling injury considerably limited my golfing activities, but this is not an excuse for me to admit that I won little in the course of my membership of Muskerry, nor indeed did I win anything in any other golf-club either. There was one exception, in the early 1950s, when I won a competition for which I suffered the usual loss of a stroke. That brought my handicap to 17, at which it has remained ever since.

Incidentally, I should mention that Máirín, my wife, did much better with fewer opportunities. She won Jerry Ryan's President's Prize in 1954.

Perhaps some of the occasions I enjoyed best were the annual 'Lads vs Chaps' matches which were organised by Frank Casey and Jim McCarthy. I would hope some time that these matches could be revived although perhaps they would have less meaning now that the GAA ban has been abolished.

One thing I always felt about Muskerry was the great *esprit de corps* that existed amongst the members. This was not confined to the golf course during the very happy socials we used to have after the various important events such as the President's and Captain's prize days, but extended into daily life activities as well.

It was a great privilege for me to have been elected President of the club in 1970, but I'm afraid I was unable, because of official commitments, to contribute much to that office. I am also very grateful to the members for having elected me an Honorary Life Member. As such, I find myself in the company of men like Mick Power and Larry McCarthy, though not for the same reason.'

Pat Stakelum's Captain's prize.
Hurlers' golf outing to Thurles, June 1975.

Front row: *J. Golden, M. Ryan, P. Barry, G. Carey, D. Garvey, P. Stakelum, B. Maher.*

Centre row: *M. Mackey, M. Hayes, J. Lynch, J. Young, B. O'Herlihy, F. Crowley, M. Dwane, P. Barry.*

Back row: *T. Shaughnessy, D. Kelly, C. Madigan, P. Curran, M. Ryan, D. Murphy, M. Murphy, B. Hoey, N. Byrne, T. Glynn, M. Henchy, S. Lynch, B. O'Shea, T. Maloney, S. Leonard, T. Ryan, R. Ryan, B. Stakelum, G. Kinnane, Fr L. Kelly, Fr R. Reidy, T. O'Connell, P.J. Garvan, J. Kennedy, M. Duggan, P. Kennedy, P. Finn, P. Lawless.*

Jack Lynch and Skibbereen Golf Club

Elected club patron in 1981

The Jack Lynch Golf Classic commenced in 1985 and remains the focal point of the club's calendar since.

A set of Jack Nicklaus golf clubs presented by US President Richard Nixon to Jack, are proudly on display in the club premises.

1987 Jack Lynch Golf classic at Skibbereen club. Jack presents his prize to Dr Michael O'Herlihy, Captain of the winning team.

Front row: *Paul Horgan, Declan O'Herlihy, Jack Kenneally.*

Back row: *Charlie McCarthy, Michael McMahon, Dr Michael O'Herlihy, Jack Lynch, Dan Walsh.*

21

A Painful Retirement

Paddy Barry
(Glen Rovers team-mate and long-time friend of Jack)

J ACK WAS DIFFERENT from many of the Mon boys who came to the club. There was always a little rivalry between the Blackpool lads and the boys who came along from the Mon. We all had our own friends but Jack mixed with everyone. From his youngest days, he was an outstanding talent. By the time he was 17, he was a big strapping young 'fella'. He was like a reindeer running, had great speed and unbelievable strength. Everyone in the club looked up to him. He had a great knowledge of the game and even when he was a youngster, selectors would seek his advice and opinion.

He played in every game he was picked for. He never sought an excuse to be absent even though he might have played a number of games in a matter of days. He loved the Glen and Ahane games which were played on a regular basis when the clubs were the Cork and Limerick champions. He used to recall a humorous story about the 'suit-lengths' final played in Milford in 1939. There was tremendous rivalry with Mick Mackey at the height of his powers at the time. The Glen were winning and a major row developed. Fr Punch ran on to the field and confronted the 'Ceann', the Glen chairman, Willie O'Connor. 'I am surprised at your carry on,' he said. 'If you don't go away Father,' the 'Ceann' said, 'you'll be even more surprised.'

**Jack Lynch and Jim Young lead out the Glen and New York
teams at Gaelic Park in 1966.**

When Jack came to New York on official business in 1952, I brought him up
to Gaelic Park to see Cork playing Galway. I persuaded him to tog off and
play, which he did. I got the gear for him and he went on, got a few nice
scores and Cork won. We celebrated into the night and he complained of
feeling sore and was told that he would be okay in the morning. He went
home by liner on the Tuesday and spent the journey in bed. The doctor on
board found that he had broken two ribs. This certainly put a painful end
to his illustrious sporting career.

**Glen Rovers at the United Nations in New York 1966 being
welcomed by the Irish Ambassador, Con Cremin.**

Left to Right: *B. O'Connell, S. O'Hanlon (UN), D.O'Neill, S. French, J. Casey,
J. Daly, J. O'Sullivan, C. Cremin, J. Lynch, T. O'Sullivan (UN), L. Ó Tuama, D. Moore,
F. O'Neill, A. O'Flynn, P. McCarthy, B. Hackett, D. Coughlan, F. Healy, C. Doolan,
C.O'Callaghan.*

Captains' Corner

Congratulating Tony Wall (Glen Rovers), captain, Féile na nGael Champions at Croke Park 1982. Paddy Buggy, Uachtarán CLCG, presents the Christy Ring trophy.

Captains of the Decades Banquet, 1987.

Paudie Ó Sé, football captain of the1980s, Jack Lynch, hurling captain of the 1940s and Mick O'Connell, football captain of the 1950s.

The Laughing Captains.

Thurles Centenary Year 1984. Jack tells Noel that it's harder to win a football All-Ireland. Noel Skehan (captain '72) played in eight All-Ireland finals, winning six; Jack Lynch (captain '42) played in eight finals winning six; Eddie Keher (captain '69) played in ten finals also winning six.

Tomás Mulcahy and Jack celebrate the 1990 All-Ireland victory.

Winning captains of Cork's four-in-a-row. Seán Condon '44, Jack Lynch '42, Connie Buckley '41, and Mick Kennefick '43.

Martin O'Doherty receives his All-Star award in 1978.

JACK LYNCH
21, GARVILLE AVENUE,
RATHGAR,
DUBLIN 6.

Mr Denis Allen
Captain
Cork Football All Ireland
Champions

19th Sept 1989

Dear Denny

Congratulations to you
your team, team manager and selectors
on a great victory last Sunday.
I was seldom if ever more thrilled
at a match or more delighted at the
outcome. It was a just reward for a
great football team. Please convey
to them my congratulations. I was
really pleased for them and especially
for you.
It was a heroic display by
Mayo - so sad they had to be on the
losing side in such a sporting game. But we
all have been there before.
I was sorry that I could not
attend the Dinner in the Royal Marine
Hotel on Sunday night.

Yours sincerely,
Jack Lynch

22

Down Through The Years

Jack Talks to Mick Dunne, RTE Radio
Interview, 27 September 1982

M.D. Tell me about the '39 final – that was a day to remember, not only for the thunder and lightning, but it also happened to be the day war was declared.

J.L. Yes, it's one of those days we'll remember for a lot of reasons, I suppose. The main reason is that it had been Cork's first final since 1931. We had been looking forward to it for a long time, and strangely enough, without diverting too much, it had a lot in common with this year's final, Kilkenny vs Cork. We went to see Kilkenny play Galway in Birr in the semi-final, and thought we were well over them, and went out certainly with an air of confidence if not with complacency. We were beaten by a point. I remember it for a lot of reasons. We were brought out to a hotel in Monkstown the night before to get us away from the madding throng, to the Saltee Hotel, now no longer in existence. The following morning when we went to Mass in Monkstown parish church, it was lashing rain. We went on to Croke Park then – it was still raining, and during the course of the day, the sun came out shining brilliantly, hailstones fell, we had thunder and lightning, and we were beaten by the proverbial one point by Kilkenny. And as I say, it was Cork's first appearance in an All-Ireland final since the famous one of 1931, and we were hoping for a breakthrough. I don't think Cork had been out of an All-Ireland final in hurling for such a long time.

M.D. It certainly was an unusually long gap.

J.L. Yes, I think we were fairly weak, and at that time they were juggling with the idea of having the County Champions select a team with a few additions from other teams. They tried it one year but it wasn't acceptable. Jim Barry went out of favour, and I think it was in 1938 that it got back to an even keel again, but we were beaten by Waterford. We had to put the bit between our teeth from 1939 onwards.

M.D. What are your memories of the thunder and lightning? Was it as bad as people now write about it? It seems to have been a ferocious storm.

1939, Cork's All-Ireland final team.

Front row: *B. Thornhill, J. Lynch (Capt.), A. Lotty, B. Ryng, W. Tabb, W. Campbell, M. Brennan, J. Young.*

Back row: *C. Buckley, J. Barrett, W. Murphy, B. Dineen, J. Quirke, J. Puttman, T. O'Sullivan, J. Barry.*

J.L. Yes, it was a raging storm, and the rain came down like stair rods. At times, it was impossible to see more than 20 yards away from you.

Conditions were almost unplayable. The ground conditions themselves were very difficult, and we felt a bit strange, as we had not been to Croke Park before, at least not as a senior county hurling team. Kilkenny had been there many times and they seemed to settle in far more quickly. They took us by surprise in the first half. I remember it for a lot of instances myself. Towards the end of the game, I got a little push from behind – I think it was Jimmy Kelly. I was about to tackle Paddy Phelan, and with the push in the back, I fell in on top of him, and a free was given against me. The free was taken by Paddy Phelan himself, and it went right towards the goal, and was just about to pass the right-hand upright. Batt Thornhill told me that Seánie O'Brien just knocked it over the line, and the umpire gave a 'seventy'. Then to add to the problem, the 'seventy' was taken and three of us got under it. The ball was heavy and didn't get in very near the goal, and Jim Young was on my left. I was just directly under it and Jack Barrett was just ahead, so I shouted, "I have it", to Barrett. Barrett mustn't have heard me, or else didn't trust me, but he leaned too far back with the result that he almost over-balanced, put his stick to it, and barely touched it. Three of us pounced on it, but Jimmy Kelly got it through for a point. The leading point, as we thought. We were convinced there were a few more minutes left, but they weren't played.

M.D. In fact, in his reminiscence, Micheál Ó Hehir maintains that the 'seventy' was taken from the wrong line.

J.L. Well, now, I didn't know that. Maybe it was because the rain was so heavy; I didn't see where the taker was standing. There was another incident in that game I'll never forget – the time when I got a pass right in front of the goal. I was right half-forward, Micka Brennan was going up the left wing and I ran in towards the centre of the goal. Micka drew the full back, and I had left my man behind me. The ball came right across in front of the square but just exactly on the line, and I hit it on the ground, angling the hurley downwards to make sure I wouldn't skew it over the bar. That's exactly what happened. I remember Jimmy O'Connell, the Kilkenny goalkeeper, looking around the back of the net for the ball, and then when he saw the white flag going up he looked around and kind of laughed at me, as if to say, 'You didn't expect that one!' or something. So there were a lot of little incidents like that, but these are incidents that one remembers.

M.D.   It was one of the instances of Kilkenny beating Cork by this extraordinary one point – they did that on many occasions.

J.L.   They did. In fact, I was on the receiving end twice – on that occasion, and again in 1947, although we had beaten them in 1946 by 4 goals. Somehow, they had a great tenacity, as they proved most spectacularly in this year's All-Ireland final, and it was always very difficult to beat them on a wet day. They had such great ball control, more so than many other counties. That's one of their great assets.

M.D.   Do you think they have this all-round skill in every generation?

J.L.   I do. I have been watching them for a very long time, and I genuinely thought this present Cork team had tremendous talent. I thought the quality of their hurling as a team, on the whole, was as good, if not better, as any I've ever seen, but the Kilkenny fellows were able to match their keenness as well, and they were sharper. They more than matched Cork in that respect, and that's what won it for Kilkenny.

M.D.   On that September day in 1939, did the fact that war was declared really impinge on the consciences of the crowd around Croke Park, or was the All-Ireland the only thing that mattered? (War had been declared before the match started.)

J.L.   That's right, and in fact, I believe Mr de Valera called a special meeting of the Dáil late that morning, and I remember some of my former TD colleagues mentioning that the meeting was over soon enough to come to Croke Park.

M.D.   I suppose the spectators wouldn't have been conscious of the catastrophe that the war was going to turn out to be.

J.L. They didn't, of course. It was probably one of those things, and we hadn't had war since 1918, and that was 20 years before. Nobody expected that there would be a repetition of the 1914–18 war. Then the catastrophe that did occur impinged on our minds, because it made hurling, and travelling to hurling matches very difficult, and one thing it caused for us was a cancellation of a tour to the US which we were to be given whether we won or lost, so unfortunately none of that Cork team ever got to America on a tour.

M.D. And the emergency years, as they are called, they were the great years of your four in a row – the travel was restricted, and people were travelling on bicycles and all…

J.L. Oh, I remember, and I think the attendances were very high. I often passed scores of fellows on the road from Cork to Limerick, Cork to Thurles, and when I was living in Dublin, from Dublin to Thurles. A funny thing in those days was that participants were entitled to travel in a taxi, but nobody else was allowed. I remember driving from Dublin to Thurles alone in a taxi, and some of my friends, my colleagues on the Civil Service hurling team, many of whom were Cork people, were cycling. I met some of them around Portlaoise, and there I was, sitting in my glory. It was a silly thing. There was no reason why they shouldn't have sat in with me if I was permitted to go.

M.D. It was the same amount of petrol. There was also the famous pony and trap. Nobody thought any the worse of anyone for going to a match in a pony and trap.

J.L. Well, one of the first games I ever played, was in a Harty Cup match, and it was in Charleville. The railway station in Charleville was a good distance away. I was playing with North Mon at the time – in the mid '30s – and all the Charleville boys came to the station and drove us the two miles to the pitch. Then we played the game. It was a great memory.

M.D. The four-in-a-row victories in the actual All-Ireland finals – it was Dublin in three, and then Antrim in that year of enormous sensation, when they beat Kilkenny up in Corrigan Park. Did it ever strike you since, that you would have loved to have beaten Kilkenny, or even Wexford? Of course, Dublin were the top team, or one of them at the time.

1944 All-Ireland final.

Cork vs Dublin. Joe Kelly goes for goal watched by Jim Donegan.

J.L.   Yes, they were one of the top teams, and at that time, I remember it well, there was a big influx of army personnel. In fact some of the army personnel we played against were Corkmen. But yes, I agree, we didn't have the satisfaction of beating Kilkenny in those days. Wexford, strangely enough, didn't come into prominence.

M.D.   No, they weren't really around.

J.L.   No, they didn't come until I was about to retire. I'll never forget the time that we went to Enniscorthy, to play them in a league match. It would have been '49 or '50, and I hadn't realised the impact Wexford were going to make in that decade, and later, when we were beaten in the National League. I assumed that it was because myself and some others were getting old, and 'twas about time to get out! But Wexford certainly heralded that they were on the way at that time.

M.D. I don't want to take from the glory of your great four-in-a-row, because the fact is we had marvellous games with great Limerick teams on the way out of Munster, and with Tipperary as well – you know, there were so many great players on those teams.

J.L. Well, my greatest memories of those were our games against Limerick, who were at their best in those days, and we had some tremendous games with them in the early '40s – marvellous games. I always remember many a tussle I had with Mick Mackey, and when I was asked to comment on his death recently, I did mention that he always gave it tough, and took it, and he hit you hard, and if you were fool enough to be in the way, that was your business. There was always a kind of smile on his face when he would do things.

M.D. You would always have the impression from listening to people, that he was a trickster, a sort of rascal on the field.

J.L. I'd say, yes he was a rascal. I wouldn't say he was a trickster, although some tricks have been attributed to him: one by Seán Ó Siocháin, of running off with the ball without dodging it on his stick, but having it in his hand. I'm inclined to believe that.

M.D. Well of course, you won all of those four All-Ireland Finals very handsomely. You won by quite big margins.

J.L. We did. We had a very good team. It was a good all-round balanced team, and as well as that – well, we can't say we hadn't stars when we had people like Christy Ring, John Quirke and Jim Young – but no one man seemed to be any better than the other men on the team. I think the biggest asset that the team had was the ability to find some resources when, inevitably, some people had off-days and we used to be able to find some other resource: it might be Jim Young one day, John Quirke another day, or Alan Lotty. Those men would always do something to lift the whole team, and this was, I think, the strength of that team.

M.D.   Of course, in that period, Ring, although the great hurler that he was, wasn't the dominant personality of Cork teams as he was, say in the '50s.

J.L.   No, he wasn't, and one would expect that a man in his early twenties would have come to his best. Well now, I wouldn't like to presume to say that he was playing with better men when he was at his best. He probably matured, although I don't know if you could say Christy Ring matured, because he was always a hurler since the day he was born practically, but he probably got more experience and was able to read the game better. Also, I suppose his reputation was building up in our time, therefore there were a lot of factors – psychological, experience and others, that made him the dominant character in the '50s.

M.D.   What was your reaction when you heard the news that Kilkenny had been beaten in Corrigan Park in 1943? I'm sure you must have been expecting to meet Kilkenny in the final.

J.L.   We were indeed. I remember when we went training soon after that, there were reports in the press about Antrim's secret weapon, but nobody could define what the secret weapon was. And I remember Jim Barry, when he brought us together the first night for training, before the All-Ireland final, he said, 'Now, we don't know what the secret weapon is, but the only weapon we have is hurling, and fitness, and this is what you're going to produce'. I don't know really what the secret weapon was, except perhaps, I played in Corrigan Park one time, and as far as I remember, standing under the post at one goal end, you couldn't see the goal at the other end.

M.D.   That's right, it's downhill all the way.

J.L.   Maybe that was the secret weapon. I don't know. As it happened, the result was very one-sided and we really felt sorry for Antrim. It's an awful feeling after a match to feel sorry for your opponent, because well, you don't want to beat them off the field. On the other hand, you don't want to pretend you're not trying. So it's a funny experience, the first I ever had and especially in an All-Ireland final. I suppose they still had problems up there, even though it was 1943, and I know one or two of them told me that it wasn't easy for them to go training, because I won't say they were obstructed, but they weren't facilitated by the powers that be.

All-Ireland final, 1943.

Jimmy Walsh, Antrim and Mick Kennefick, Cork lead out the teams.

M.D. Well, maybe Kilkenny had problems travelling up, or problems with complacency.

J.L. Well that's the one and nothing else. I just couldn't believe the result, and we went to Croke Park with some apprehension of what the secret weapon might be. It proved to be nothing really.

M.D. You've mentioned Jim Barry there a few times, and I know from talking to former Cork hurlers of your own era, and afterwards, that everybody who passed through Jim Barry's hands, all Cork hurlers had a great affection for him, and yet he was this extraordinary person. He wasn't a former All-Ireland player himself, in fact, if he played, it was moderate club hurling.

J.L. I think he was a junior hurler with Blackrock in his day. Not only did he not play, but also I wouldn't ascribe to Jim a very in-depth knowledge of all the aspects of hurling. He had a tremendous ability to bring out the best in the team he was training. He used to do everything. When the training session started, he would go down to the Park to make sure the grass was cut. If it wasn't, he would kick up holy murder. He'd make sure the jerseys were washed and the towels were washed. If somebody was doing work, it might be a traveller, or somebody on shift work, where the job would take up time when he should be training, Jim would go to the boss – the very managing director – and insist that this man be left off. After matches, win or lose, he always made sure that the team were sitting down to a good meal, and he wouldn't let anybody interfere. You know – the welfare of the team in every respect. And Jim was generous. He hadn't a lot of money, but I know he made what little he had available to people who were in trouble, I mean ordinary financial embarrassment, temporary financial embarrassment. So, he had a lot of characteristics that made one like him, and respect him. And all these put together, his enthusiasm particularly, tended to bring the best out of the team.

M.D. And I think the County Board bowed to him in a sense. I remember going to training sessions, and there was always an air of banter afterwards. Jim being the father figure, was in fact often the butt of a lot of the jokes and banter from the players. It always appeared to me that the County Board members weren't terribly welcome there, and they let Jim get on with the business of training.

J.L. Absolutely! As a matter of fact during my period, I don't think I ever met the selection committee or if I did, it was very seldom. Naturally, they would go to training sessions, but somehow they didn't seem to get near the team, and whether Jim protected us from them or them from us, I don't know. He certainly had tremendous influence, and of course chairmen came and went: the great Bowler Walsh, Henry O'Mahony, and all those people, but there was one constant there all the time – Seán Óg Murphy. I think Seán Óg had a very high regard for Jim Barry, but only as long as he felt Barry was doing his job. Seán was as tough and relentless as anybody can be in his job, so I think that was one of the great assets of the team, and of the whole system then. There was a great understanding between Seán Óg Murphy and Jim Barry.

M.D. But, of course, you were all so talented on that team anyhow, and I'm not taking from Jim's powers of reading the game or training, but you got down to it. You hadn't much else to do; in fact, you didn't have many counter-attractions.

J.L. No! When you say we were all talented, we had our quota of talent, but we had our weaknesses too, and some of us knew them better than anybody. I suppose we know our own personal weaknesses and sometimes we mightn't be able to hide them. There weren't many counter-attractions, especially during the war years. We all went training night after night, cycling, some from Fermoy, Mitchelstown and Midleton. Con Murphy and Jack Barrett from the South East came by car, but they were hired cars mainly. I don't think any of our team owned a car.

Also, I think that talent came from our school days, because on our half-day, well in my school anyway in the North Mon, we always went up to the Mon Field to practise, and there was a little field in front of the Brothers' residence (not a very good one) but we used to knock about there as well, and we enjoyed nothing more than that, so we were kind of living hurling all the time.

M.D. And, of course, cycling in itself was helping towards the fitness too.

J.L. Indeed, I'm sure it was, and we cycled to many a game – not so much with the Cork Team – although I remember one time getting a lift on the crossbar of a bike out to Ballincollig to play a game, and when I got off the crossbar, I thought I had no legs! I had to soften out. There was great commitment, though that's not to detract from the young lads today. There must be commitment because they are producing a high quality of hurling and football, and I think this year proved it. And also they are probably fitter, I don't know, possibly fitter than we were. But I'd like to see that tested.

M.D. Let's get on to 1945 then, the year you got your football medal – there is a story that you nearly didn't get to Croke Park for that final, which was against Cavan.

J.L. In fact, that's quite right, and I thought I had lost my chance. Jim Hurley was on the selection committee. He was a great Cork hurling midfielder. A native of Clonakilty, of course, which was, and still is, a great football stronghold. He was in the local government service, and then he became Secretary of UCC, and it was while he was in UCC that he became a selector for the Cork football team. For some reason or other, he felt I deserved my place. I suppose it's as much for field-craft ability rather than football ability. I was doing my Bar finals in that year and I was in digs in Terenure in Dublin, which wasn't far from the 16-bus route. This went right beside Croke Park, down under the railway bridge, and on to the road out to Drumcondra. I met the boys from the team in the hotel in Dublin the night before, and we usually foregathered on the morning of the game, for a cup of tea and maybe a pep talk. I told Jim Barry that there was no need for me to go to that as I was living 30 yards from the bus, and that I'd be there in good time. So I did that. I went to the bus queue near Kenilworth Square. Several full buses passed, and there was a big queue. I was getting a bit worried, looking at my watch – of course, it didn't occur to me at that time to get a taxi. I was surprised that so many people from that area seemed to be going to the football final and after a while, when I got really worried, I broke the queue and stepped on the platform of the bus. The bus conductor put up his hand and said 'Oh no you don't, you have to take your turn'. 'Look', I said, 'I'm playing in the All-Ireland final today'. 'Oh,' he said, 'that's about the best one I ever heard. Stay on.' Obviously, he thought it was such a good one, he decided to give in to me. Anyway I got there, and ran around the back of the Cusack Stand from the main Drumcondra Road, and came around by the dressing rooms. There seemed to be a deathly silence inside except for the sound of someone pacing up and down in the dressing room. Hesitantly, I knocked on the door. It was Jim Hurley who happened to be pacing up and down the floor, with nerves I suppose. He opened the door and he looked at me, and I thought he was going to savage me. He said, 'Hello Jack Lynch, you were great to come'.

M.D. Do you think he was being sarcastic?

J.L. No, I don't think so, because, I remember him using that phrase before when, during the war years we'd pass a plethora of cyclists on our way to a match and Jim would say, 'Aren't they great to come'. So I think it was a kind of impulsive, natural statement Jim made.

M.D. What can you remember from that All-Ireland Championship campaign in football?

J.L. Well, I remember early on I was playing in Dublin with the Civil Service team, and I was lucky to have won a Dublin County Championship with them. I was playing with a good team so I suppose favourable reports of my displays were going back to Cork, and I played in the first round of the Munster Championship against Tipperary. We didn't do too well. We were lucky enough to win. For the second game, the Munster final in Killarney, I didn't think my appearance in Killarney was all that important, and I didn't want to create a fuss. I knew Paddy Kennedy, who was also living in Dublin, and went down with him. The Kerry fellows were very complacent and felt that this was a small chore they had to do to get them to the semi-final. As it happened, I was playing right corner-forward. The first two balls came down. I let fly from a good distance out and got two points. I seemed to justify my selection, but nobody was more surprised than I was to see the balls going over the bar. So I think that was sufficient for me to retain my place right into the final. It was Galway we beat in the semi-final, and we played Cavan in the final. I remember well, I had an unfortunate incident with big Tom O'Reilly, and a lot of Cavan people believed I had hit him deliberately, and I think it's worth detailing what happened for the record. I was playing inside Mick Tubridy at right corner-forward, Mick was right half-forward, and I found myself further down the field than I should be. Tubridy got possession and I ran up inside him, maybe 30 to 40-yards out from the goal. Knowing I was out of my position and knowing Mick Tubridy never hit a ball unless he knew exactly what he wanted to do with it – pass it or score – I ran up past and inside Mick, with my head turned right, watching what he was going to do with the ball. Next thing I felt a shadow coming on my left. I turned around quickly, and the bone behind my left ear hit whoever I had run into over the right eye, and it was Big Tom O'Reilly, and we both went down. I got up fairly quickly. Big Tom was hurt a bit all right, but I was accused afterwards of tripping him and kicking him on the head while he was on the ground.

M.D.   Cavan people will never believe anything else.

J.L.   I suppose they won't – they may still believe it. I often met Big Tom afterwards in Leinster House, and I said 'Tom, did you ever straighten the record? (Big Tom was a TD in the early days when I was a TD in 1948), and he said 'I did, but they don't believe me'.

M.D.   These stories sort of grow as the years go on and probably in part of Cavan you were known as the man who knocked out Big Tom.

J.L.   Yes, well and that's the exact story, and I was very annoyed afterwards that they didn't believe me.

M.D.   For the sixth All-Ireland medal – and you're the only man to have six in succession – we go back to Kilkenny, the team that you didn't meet in that four-in-a-row, and you met them in the two-in-a-row, '46 and '47. You beat them in '46.

J.L.   We beat them, and beat them well in '46. I think there were three goals as a margin, but we had a very good evenly-balanced team on that day. We had Con Murphy, Alan Lotty, Jim Young, Seán Condon, the Riordans (Gerry and Mossie) and Joe Kelly in the forward line. And Joe Kelly, of course, was like a greyhound. He was the 100-yards champion of Ireland. I think Joe used to course the ball around, outstrip the backline from the left corner – that's where he was playing – right around almost to the right corner, outstripping everybody, and then banging it into the back of the net. So we had a very good team that day, and we won it well, as you say. Ring of course was just coming to the height of his fame. That was the day he got a tremendous goal from about half-way out in one of the most spectacular solo runs I've ever seen. So all round it was a very good display. Perhaps Kilkenny were taken by surprise. They were probably not as good as they were the following year, but strangely enough, even though it was my sixth in a row, I wasn't terribly conscious of that fact until later when I read about it in the weeks that followed.

I suppose people weren't conscious of it, or reporters didn't highlight it, but naturally enough I was delighted, as I was the previous year when I got the football medal after the four-in-a-row hurling medals.

1946 All-Ireland team.

Dan O'Rourke, President of the GAA, throws in the ball between Christy Ring and Dan Kennedy. Con Cottrell, Jack Lynch and Gerry Riordan are ready for action.

M.D. The following year then, I suppose, it must be fair to say you were fairly confident going out again against Kilkenny in the final.

J.L. We were, and I think that was won by a little bit of luck, as are most games that are won by the narrowest of margins although people say you make your own luck. But on those occasions, little things happen, the break of the ball, etc., and I remember Kilkenny used to have the habit of running many more steps with the ball in the hand than we did, and they seemed to be getting away with it. Towards the end of the game I had a chance. I saw an opening and saw that if I could get inside the man in front of me I could get within 20 yards of the goal. I was fairly well bottled up on either side, so I ran about 5 steps, got in, and just as I was about to hit for goal, the whistle blew against me. I was fairly annoyed, because I believe Kilkenny fellows were getting away with longer runs but then, be that as it may, towards the end there was pressure on the backs. Jim Young got possession from a 'seventy'. He was tackled as he cleared the ball. Terry Leahy gathered it and banged it over the bar. I was always annoyed about that. Terry shouldn't have been left alone, and again, of course, the minute the ball was over the bar, that was the end of the game.

M.D. This one point defeat again.

J.L. Yes, this one point defeat. However, it was a great game. People tell me it was one of the best.

M.D. I know you have told us this story on RTÉ before, but it's worth repeating, and that is the story of your last game and what you suffered during and after it, which was, in fact, played abroad.

J.L. That's right. Well it was a competitive game but nothing to do with the GAA in Ireland. I was part of a parliamentary delegation in 1952, and I had played my last hurling game in 1950. I had been at a conference in Ottawa, and I came back via New York. I met a great friend of mine there, Paddy Barry, who was a former Glen Rovers hurler and he suggested to me that I might go to Gaelic Park on Saturday as Cork were playing that day. I said I would love to go, and I went. There were two or three other games on as well. I don't know how they operate, but some county seems to take over the field for the day, and John Kerry O'Donnell supplied the field and the beer at the end of the game for the customers. Cork were playing Galway. It was a Cork team in New York, and it didn't necessarily mean that all the players were Corkmen, and all the Galway team were from Galway. There might have been a bit of county mobility. The first game was almost coming to an end, and the Cork game was about to start and I was asked to come and meet the team. I did and they said, 'Why not tog out and play with us?' I told them it was two years since I had played, and that I had put on a bit of weight. One fellow pointed to a man in the corner, I think Buckley was his name. 'Look at him, He's about 40!' I was in my thirties at this stage this time, so after some more persuasion I said okay, I'd line out for ten minutes. So having fulfilled my contract, I lay down after 10 minutes, but they said to keep going. I said I would for another 10 minutes, and it went on like this until half-time. They tried to persuade me to play on, by saying 'We're right in the game, the wind is behind us, we have a chance.' I repeated the dose (the 10 minutes). I wanted to come off as I wasn't feeling too well. Anyway in the last couple of minutes I hit a ball, and I was watching it to see if it was going wide or barely wide or barely inside the goal. Just as the ball was going to land, I got a charge with a hurley in the ribs. I went down in some pain.

The following day I came home. I had flown out, and had decided to come back by boat for the experience on the *Nieuw Amsterdam*. It was the flagship of the Holland-America fleet. It was a small boat by Atlantic standards, and it happened to be a very rough crossing. The boat was like the Holy Ground boat, 'the good old ship was tossing about' and I was getting pain in my ribs with every movement it made. Eventually, I went into my bunk and I asked for the ship's doctor to come. I don't think he was a highly-qualified man, but he did, fair play to him, diagnose broken ribs, and he put one of those gauze bandages about two inches around me, and gave me a shot of morphine or something. It wasn't nearly strong enough, so I was tossing around in the bunk. When I woke up the next morning I was really hurt because the bandage had rolled itself into a kind of whipcord and I was cut to pieces as well as being sore inside. That was the last hurling match I ever played, and I'm hardly likely to play one like it again!

M.D. And one you will certainly remember.

J.L. Indeed, I will.

M.D. Jack, thank you very much. It's been great talking to you again.

23

Accept Victory
With Modesty

Thanksgiving Service for the Gift of Sport

At the Church of the Sacred Heart,
Donnybrook, Dublin, March 1983

'If you play games you are likely to be hurt in your pride as well as in your body. This probably is not the most appropriate way to open an address on an occasion such as this, but knowing that the great majority here present are actively interested and are or have been participants in sports, I feel that you will appreciate the truth of this assertion. Time will cure most hurts whether of mind or of body.

One's pride is hurt by missing a two-foot putt in golf, failing to hit a close-up free or penalty in hurling or rugby between the posts, or losing a game against little fancied opponents. These things happen

to the greatest athletes, players and teams in the world. In this respect, involvement in sport is an antidote to pride, a controller of impulse, and a great chastener. It imposes self-restraint and, therefore, it is a builder of character.

Whenever I was lax in my application to study while at school, I took refuge in the old Latin tag 'Mens sana in corpore sano'. I chose to interpret this as an admonition that if I wanted to make the best use of what brains the Good Lord gave me, I had to keep fit. Jogging as it is understood and practised nowadays, was unknown when I was a young adult so we convinced ourselves that the only way to have a healthy mind and be fit, was by training, and only for the purpose of competitive sport. I must admit, however, that fellows in my class who attained academic distinction in later life and became university professors, ambassadors, secretaries of departments of State, and even poets of renown showed no propensity to develop a 'corpus sanum' by playing games. Perhaps they were the exceptions that proved the rule, and even if they were not, I am still convinced that participation in sport is essential to the forming of the whole man or woman.

In this the international youth year, there can be no more important code of behaviour, no more significant doctrine for wholesome living that we can transmit to young people than that of involvement in sport. As in games, there will inevitably be, in the course of their lives, successes and setbacks, achievements and disappointments. In the playing of games and athletic combat, young people are encouraged to play hard but fair, to accept victory with modesty and defeat with grace. The experience of earnest and honourable combat in sport and acceptance of the result without harbouring any sense of rancour towards opponents when the game is over, are valuable lessons that young people can learn from sport which they can apply in later years. Through participation in sport, young people will have inculcated in them a sense of discipline and respect for authority. Goodness knows, nothing is more needed nowadays in our young and not so young people.

All of this will not come to our young players and athletes simply by active participation in sport without guidance and without having imparted to them the highest standards. And who better to give that guidance than people like you, who have yourselves been involved in sport. Many of you did just that. You gave that guidance and the benefit of your experience in your respective sports to young participants. There are also many, and I do not exclude myself from this category, who do not involve ourselves sufficiently in the sports activities of succeeding generations, and who, to use the cliché, do not put back into the game what we ourselves got out of it. Young players must be encouraged to practise good sportsmanship, and taught that regardless of how important each game is, and each match or contest, whether a friendly game, league or championship, the winning of it is not the be-all and end-all of living. One of the most important roles that sport is playing in Ireland today is that of promoting good will and understanding between North and South. All-Ireland central authorities control most of our major spectator sports and of our lesser ones, and their teams that represent Ireland in international competition are selected on an all-Ireland basis.

We may well be on the verge of international Gaelic football, limited though it may be to matches against Australian teams. We may know in the next few years if there is a future for it. If there is, our team will represent all Ireland.

The game that comes quickly to mind especially at this time of year that facilitates North-South competition and whose international team represents the whole island, is rugby. Irish people, North and South, irrespective of religious or political persuasion are always proud to see Ireland do well in rugby internationals. It is self-evident that an all-Ireland soccer team could put us in contention for European and World cup honours in future years. As things are, it is difficult for two separate teams representing at international level, two parts of an island with a total population of 5 million people, to compete successfully with countries who have ten and twenty times our population. It is obvious that participation at that level is for the 'greats', but young people will always look up to the 'greats' in their different sports and though only the few will attain their standards, they will always aspire to attain them. Whether they achieve that kind of success or not, regardless of how indifferent or unobtrusive their playing careers may be, sportsmen and women are able to establish an affinity and camaraderie between each other that last their lifetime, more so than is experienced in almost any other sphere of human activity.

A friendship with sports and sports people is a friendship for life, a friendship that transcends political boundaries and religious divides.'

24

A Great Childhood Hero

To us as youngsters listening to what was being discussed around us about hurling, it seemed that Jack Lynch was just as important as the nightly rosary and took second place only to God. The 'ructions' always started before the game commenced in the garden: a toss-up first, which of us was going to be Jack Lynch, the loser having to be satisfied with being Mick Mackey.

There was always an 'aura' of invincibility about Jack Lynch. Whether it was Glen Rovers, St Nicks or Cork, everything had to be okay when Jack Lynch was playing. Defeat was out of the question. If it did happen, we were always told that Jack had a 'blinder'. It was all we wanted to hear.

Too young to go to the 1939 County final against Blackrock, despite earnest pleas, I can vividly remember most of the family heading off for the Cork Athletic Grounds. The Glen won their sixth county title in a row and Jack Lynch was brilliant. Great consolation for not being present. The same year, listening to the All-Ireland final between Cork and Kilkenny on the old battery radio, Cork being beaten did not seem to be important to a child. How many times Micheál Ó Hehir mentioned Jack Lynch's name was what counted.

At the first County final against 'Sars' in 1940, there we were, standing on two concrete blocks. Jack Lynch was playing and the Glen won again.

Though it was hard to see over the railings, he was there in the thick of the action. We had seen our hero for the first time. This was a dream come true.

We were back again for the 1941 final against Ballincollig – another victory. Eight county championships in a row. Eight medals for Jack. A five-mile walk home, but no complaints. The same year, Jack won the first of four hurling All-Ireland medals in a row for Cork. He was captain in 1942, and we cut out the magnificent photos from the papers and put them safely away.

One Sunday in the summer of 1943, he was playing football against Kerry in the Munster Championship at the Cork Athletic Grounds. Of course, we had forgotten, or maybe were never told, that he had already won two Minor, one Intermediate and two Senior football championship medals with St Nicks. The match was a draw and there was great excitement. We were back again for the replay, into the sideline – the nearest we had ever been to our 'hero'. Victory for Cork, the shock of the century, and there he was in front of us, being carried along on the shoulders of big grown men.

Two years later, 1945, Cork and Kerry played in the Munster final. Cork were victorious and it was followed by the first football All-Ireland victory since 1911 and Jack was the toast of the county. Cork and Jack had won five All-Irelands in a row. 1946 saw another hurling win for Cork against Kilkenny. Jack Lynch was record-making and record-breaking as we were getting older.

In the sixties and seventies, it was my pleasure as secretary of Glen Rovers to invite Jack to various club functions and advise him of important activities, as he was a Trustee of the club. If ever a Glen function clashed with more important engagements, he always requested us to try for an alternative date, which he would suggest, and this we were always happy to do.

1977, Glen Rovers All-Ireland Club Champions' victory dinner.

From left: Jack Lynch, Alice Ó Tuama, Máirín Lynch, Liam Ó Tuama.

Ministerial duties curtailed his visits to Blackpool, but in 1966, the Golden Jubilee year of the Club, a tour of Boston, Chicago and New York was organised. The week we visited New York, Jack was attending a meeting of the World Bank. He was at the game between New York and the Glen at Gaelic Park, and came along to the celebration party after the game, with his New York-based friends, Joe Looney and Paddy Barry. He sang the 'Boston Burgler' and 'Roses of Picardy' to the delight of what seemed to be hundreds of Blackpool Americans. Next morning, he accompanied the tour party to the United Nations, where we were all welcomed by the Irish Ambassador, Con Cremin, in a most lavish manner.

There were very many more happy memories over the years. In 1974, he launched the club history, *The Spirit of The Glen* which I compiled, and in

July 1997, I was invited to his house to represent Glen Rovers for the presentation of his medals to the Croke Park Museum. These were accepted by Liam Mulvihill, Director General of the GAA in the presence of Con Murphy and some close friends. This was a very special day for Jack.

Presentation to Rev. Fr Paddy Barry (Captain of Glen Rovers County Champions, 1976) on his ordination.

Front row: *Rev. Fr O'Callaghan, T. McCarthy, J. Lynch, L. Ó Tuama, Rev. Fr. P. Barry, E. Buckley, T. Murphy, D. O'Brien, B. Hackett.*

Back row: *D. O'Donovan, G. Holohan, N. Lynam, E. Barrett, M. McCarthy, A. Ó Tuama, D. Owens, M. O'Doherty, J. Lynam, J. Daly.*

He enjoyed every moment of it and recalled many amusing incidents which took place during his illustrious career.

The highlight of all the contacts I had with Jack Lynch through the years, came on the 12 December 1997. Glen Rovers' new sports complex was officially opened on that day, by GAA President, Joe McDonagh. Jack was unable to be present, but his wife Máirín, with whom I had regularly been in touch, was keeping him up to date with all the news from Blackpool. He was very anxious to convey his congratulations to all concerned. A telephone link was organised for 4.30pm on that day, and as club chairman, I had the great honour of putting through the call to his house. His congratulations were relayed to the 500 members and guests present.

Present at the official launching of the *Spirit of the Glen* in 1973: Christy Ring, Seán Ó Siocháin, Jack Lynch, Theo Lynch and Liam Ó Tuama.

He spoke to some of his great friends, including Paddy Barry, and when Jackie Daly sang 'The Banks' and 'Beautiful City' for him, Jack could be clearly heard joining in. This turned a day of celebration into one of sheer joy and emotion.

Jack Lynch was a man of immense stature. His skill, ability, leadership and presence on the play fields place him among the 'greats' of the GAA. His record-making achievements put him among the 'élite'. To those who knew him, he was a gentleman of extraordinary charm, kindness and courtesy. Despite attaining the status of World Statesman, he had no 'Airs and Graces' about him. Whether he was in Dáil Eireann, Downing Street, Brussels, Molly Howe's pub in Blackpool or Glen Rovers club, Jack Lynch was never out of place. He was a great childhood hero.

25

For the Record...

Jack Lynch
(1917-1999)

15 August 1917	Date of Birth
1945	Called to the Bar
10 August 1946	Married
1948	Elected to the Dáil
1951–54	Parliamentary Secretary
1957	Minister for Gaeltacht
1957–59	Minister for Education
1959–65	Minister for Industry and Commerce
1965–66	Minister for Finance
1966–1973	Taoiseach
1977–79	Taoiseach
19 December 1980	Freeman of Cork

Championship & League Victories (1929–1950)

1929: North Parish Under-16 Football Championship.

1930: North Parish Under-16 Hurling Championship, City Division, Minor Football Championship.

1931: North Parish Under-16 Hurling Championship.

1932: Cork County Minor Football Championship.

1933: Cork County Minor Football Championship. Cork County Minor Hurling Championship.

1934: Cork County Senior Hurling Championship. Cork County Minor Hurling Championship (Captain). Harty Cup Colleges Senior Hurling Championship.

1935: Cork County, Senior Hurling Championship. Harty Cup Colleges Senior Hurling Championship. Munster Colleges Senior Football Championship. Inter-Provincial Colleges Senior Hurling Championship. City Division Minor Hurling Championship (Captain). City Division Minor Football Championship.

1936: Cork County, Senior Hurling Championship. Harty Cup Colleges Senior Hurling Championship (Captain). Munster Colleges Senior Football Championship. Inter-Provincial Colleges Senior Hurling Championship (Captain).

Cork County Schools and College 120-yards Hurdles Championship (16.6 seconds)

1937: Cork County Senior Hurling Championship. Cork County Intermediate Football Championship.

1938: Cork County Senior Hurling Championship. Cork County Senior Football Championship. Inter-Provincial Railway Cup Hurling Championship.

1939: Cork County Senior Hurling Championship (Captain). Munster Senior Hurling Championship (Captain). National Hurling League (Captain). Inter-Provincial Railway Cup Hurling Championship.

1940: Cork County Senior Hurling Championship (Captain). National Hurling League (Captain). Inter-Provincial Railway Cup Hurling.

1941: All-Ireland Senior Hurling Championship. Cork County Senior Hurling Championship. Cork County Senior Football Championship.

1942: All-Ireland Senior Hurling Championship (Captain). Inter-Provincial Railway Cup Hurling Championship. Munster Senior Hurling Championship (Captain).

1943: All-Ireland Senior Hurling Championship. Inter-Provincial Railway Cup Hurling Championship (Captain). Munster Senior Hurling Championship. Munster Senior Football Championship.

1944: All-Ireland, Senior Hurling Championship. Inter-Provincial Railway Cup Hurling Championship. Munster Senior Hurling Championship. Dublin Senior Football Championship.

1945: Munster Senior Football Championship. All-Ireland, Senior Football Championship.

1946: Munster Senior Hurling Championship. All-Ireland, Senior Hurling Championship.

1947: Munster Senior Hurling Championship. Kelleher Shield Senior Football League (Captain).

1948: Cork County Senior Hurling Championship. National Hurling League.

1949: Cork County Senior Hurling Championship. Inter-Provincial Railway Hurling Cup Championship.

1950: Cork County Senior Hurling Championship.

Awards

Team of the Millennium.

Team of the Century (1984).

Texaco Hall of Fame (1984).

Hurling Captain of the Forties.

Cork Millennium Team.

Bank of Ireland All-Time Hurling Award (1981).

Jury's Hall of Fame (1983).

Championship and League
Runners-up Medals (1930–1951)

1930: Cork County, Minor Football Championship.

1932: Cork County, Minor Hurling Championship.

1933: Munster, Minor Hurling Championship.

1934: Munster, Minor Hurling Championship (Captain). Munster Minor Football Championship. Cork County Intermediate Football Championship.

1935: Munster Minor Hurling Championship (Captain). Munster Minor Football Championship. Cork County Minor Hurling Championship (Captain). Cork County Minor Football Championship.

1939: All-Ireland Senior Hurling Championship (Captain).

1940: Munster Senior Hurling Championship (Captain).

1941: Munster Senior Hurling Championship. Inter-Provincial Railway Cup Hurling Championship.

1946: Cork County Senior Hurling Championship.

1947: All-Ireland, Senior Hurling Championship. Munster Senior Football Championship. Cork County Senior Football Championship (Captain).

1948: Munster Senior Hurling Championship.

1949: National Hurling League.

1950: Munster Senior Hurling Championship.

1951: Cork County Senior Football Championship.

Jack Lynch played in 79 championship and league finals from 1929, at 12 years of age until he retired at 34 in 1951, playing only one game in that year. On that occasion, St Nicks had qualified for the Cork Senior Football Championship final and as they had a depleted team, due to injuries and suspensions, they asked him to play. He agreed to do so, and despite his lack of training and fitness, contributed greatly to the team's performance.

An Post's Team of the Millenium

Tony Reddin
(Tipperary)

Bobby Rackard
(Wexford)

Nick O'Donnell
(Wexford)

John Doyle
(Tipperary)

Brian Whelahan
(Offaly)

John Keane
(Waterford)

Paddy Phelan
(Kilkenny)

Lory Meagher
(Kilkenny)

Jack Lynch
(Cork)

Christy Ring
(Cork)

Mick Mackey
(Limerick)

Jim Langton
(Kilkenny)

Jimmy Doyle
(Tipperary)

Ray Cummins
(Cork)

Eddie Keher
(Kilkenny)

Leeside's Final Tribute

The time you won your town the game
We cheered you through the streets and lanes;
Man and boy stood cheering by,
And home we brought you shoulder high.
Today this road all players come,
Shoulder-high we bring you home.
And set you at the threshold down
Townsman now of a stiller town.

A.E. Housman